rebuilding YOUTH ministry

"When the local Church sets priorities, youth ministry nearly always rises to the top. But the solution we seem to land on generally results in a whirlwind of activities with no clear direction, offered in a dingy room, put on by someone who is too often burned out within a year and looking for 'a real job.' Youth ministry done this way is rarely taken seriously because, let's face it, it's rarely successful. Christopher Wesley offers refreshing clarity in the midst of this craziness. In a word, he offers great vision for a ministry the Church so often gets wrong but really can't afford to."

Chris Stefanick
Founder and president of Real Life Catholic

"What I love about Chris Wesley is that this isn't simply theory—he knows what he's doing and he has shared his simple and practical tools to help us build a dynamic and more effective youth ministry for our churches. This book is a gift!"

Doug Fields
Author of *Purpose Driven Youth Ministry*

"Chris Wesley has put together an inspiring, affirming, challenging, and encouraging book that is a must-read for anyone involved in youth ministry. Chris's love for both youth and youth workers oozes from the pages of this great book."

Clayton Imoo
Director, Office of Youth and Young Adult Ministry
Archdiocese of Vancouver

"Christopher Wesley provides clarity and insight into the exciting and tumultuous life and work of a person called to youth ministry. With humor and honesty, he helps shed light on the countless challenges we face and how best to form the vision each ministry program needs to be truly successful. This book should be in the hands of every person working with youth, whether a rookie or veteran!"

Katie Prejean
Youth Director, Our Lady Queen of Heaven Parish
Lake Charles, Louisiana

rebuilding YOUTH ministry

Ten Practical Strategies for Catholic Parishes

Christopher Wesley

AVE MARIA PRESS AVE Notre Dame, Indiana

To my incredible wife, Kate, and my sons, Matthew and Benjamin,
thank you for showing me God's unconditional love.
And to all the youth ministers in the trenches doing God's work.
It's totally worth it.

Scripture texts in this work are taken from the *New American Bible*, revised edition © 2010, 1991, 1986, 1970 Confraternity of Christian Doctrine, Washington, DC, and are used by permission of the copyright owner. All Rights Reserved. No part of the *New American Bible* may be reproduced in any form without permission in writing from the copyright owner.

Founded in 1865, Ave Maria Press is a ministry of the United States Province of Holy Cross.

www.avemariapress.com

Paperback: ISBN-13 978-1-59471-576-1

E-book: ISBN-13 978-1-59471-577-8

Cover and text design by Andy Wagoner.

Printed and bound in the United States of America.

Library of Congress Cataloging-in-Publication Data
Wesley, Christopher.
  Rebuilding youth ministry : 10 practical strategies for Catholic parishes / Christopher Wesley ; foreword by Tom Corcoran and Michael White.
    pages cm
  Includes bibliographical references.
  ISBN 978-1-59471-576-1 -- ISBN 1-59471-576-9
  1. Church work with youth--Catholic Church. I. Title.
  BX2347.8.Y7W47 2015
  259'.23088282--dc23
                    2014037364

CONTENTS

CONTENTS

FOREWORD

Youth ministry is often described as serving the "future Church," which is sort of right and sort of not right.

The "sort of *not* right" part is the misunderstanding that students are, at best, only the Church in training. In this view the Church is a community of adults, and the only reason we make a current investment in students is because one day they will be part of that adult community. This kind of attitude misses the vital role of youth ministry in the life of our parishes. Students, of course, are an important part of the Church *right now*. God very much desires a growing relationship with them and has granted them gifts and talents to serve him and his family.

The "sort of right" part, on the other hand, recognizes that current students are the future of the Church if the Church is to have a future. As adults we have the responsibility to pass down to the next generation the rich Tradition of our Catholic faith as well as what we have learned on our own faith journey and what God has done in our lives. Calling students the *future* Church reminds us that it is our responsibility to mentor and encourage them into a fully devoted relationship with Jesus Christ so that they in turn can lead the next generation in the future.

Both of us have had the privilege to work with Chris Wesley here at our parish for more than a decade. What we love about our student ministry program under Chris's direction is that he takes both these aspects of student ministry very seriously. Chris and the incredible team of youth leaders he has built understand the critical role of youth ministry now and for the future of our Church.

What you will find in the following pages is solid direction for effective youth ministry from a parish minister who learned these valuable lessons in the field. This book is not theory or theology; it's a field manual with incredibly practical steps you also can take toward rebuilding or building for the first time a vibrant youth ministry at your parish—one that exists to make disciples who in turn make other disciples.

Leading the next generation of students is not optional; it is fundamental and critical to building healthy parishes and to the work of the New Evangelization. Let Chris Wesley be your guide and companion in this awesome work.

Michael White and Tom Corcoran
Authors of *Rebuilt*

PREFACE

As a young teenager, I couldn't wait to plug in to my parish high school youth ministry program. Middle school youth group had been awesome, and the high school group meant new friends, fun activities, and cute high school girls—at least that's what I thought it meant. I watched my sister and my mom, a volunteer with the youth group, come home after Sunday night youth meetings filled with good stories and a lot of energy. I wanted that—wanted to be a part of it—and in the end, youth ministry had a huge impact on my teen years.

I was a struggling teenager who needed love, and I found it in my parish youth group. My parents divorced during those years, and youth ministry was an escape. It was a place where I felt supported and safe. Toward the end of my senior year, though, I was dealt a hard blow that left a decidedly sour taste in my mouth.

I was looking forward to my last retreat with our youth group, assuming I would be a peer leader on the planning team. Shortly before the retreat team was to be announced, our youth minister called me into her office and said, "Chris, we're not going to ask you to be on the team for this retreat." I was shocked and immediately begged for a reason, but I was definitely not ready for her response: "I don't think you're stable enough right now."

I was so angry and felt completely defeated. She tried to soften the blow by telling me that I was welcome to come on the retreat as a participant, but it was too late for that—I was heartbroken. I left church that night and cried. There was painful truth in her reasoning—I was not a great role model for my peers—but the experience left me crushed. I was ready to walk away—not only from youth ministry but also from the Church. I was a hurting teenager who needed the Church, especially my local parish, but all I felt was abandoned.

One would think that after such a negative experience, youth ministry would hold the bottom slot on my list of dream jobs. As a matter of fact, it wasn't on the list at all when I started making career decisions. Throughout college, though, and then during a year-long commitment with the Jesuit Volunteer Corps, God brought many opportunities and individuals into my life that gradually shaped me into a fairly successful youth minister. Although I wasn't aware of it, God was preparing me in those early years for this work. So, here I am—fifteen years after that painful ending of high school—happy and fulfilled, immersed in youth ministry.

As the director of student ministry at Church of the Nativity in Timonium, Maryland, I have lived through lonely nights when it seemed like no one else cared. Even after ten years, I still have bad days when I wonder if youth ministry is really necessary and other days when I see with crystal clear vision why this work is essential to growing God's kingdom. Nearly every day, I meet men and women who feel passionate about investing in and mobilizing our Catholic young people, but in many churches, youth ministry is low on the priority list. That is sad but not surprising. Many (perhaps most) parish leaders don't believe that teens can, let alone will, contribute financially, lead others, and act maturely and responsibly enough to contribute to the community in vital ways. If parish leaders think about young people at all, they usually consider ways to entertain them or to get their help with projects that other people have decided are good ideas. Mostly, I'm afraid the youth in our parishes are not considered much at all.

Even still, we all know that a church with young people is attractive. It has energy, vibrancy, and hope for the future. The problem is that running a youth ministry is a challenge. It's messy, and that's because adolescence is messy. Young people experience so much physical, emotional, and intellectual change. What's more, for youth ministers and adult volunteers, working around the schedules of teens and their families can be a frustrating, even daunting ordeal in and of itself.

All too often, the approach to growing a youth ministry in Catholic parishes is to hire a young college graduate with a lot of energy who will work long hours—mostly evenings and week-ends—for next to nothing. He or she is then charged with creating a program that no one will know about with a group that meets in the dark depths of the church basement. What is the result of this ill-conceived effort? Too often it is nothing but a burned-out, disconnected youth minister ready to leave for some other career, and a handful of disappointed parents with disaffected teens.

Youth ministry is far too often reduced to a caricature of babysitting, a simple matter of offering pizza and Ping-Pong so teens hang out at church rather than somewhere else—but it can and should be so much more. Effective youth ministry is the coming together of the present and future of the Church. It's the movement that takes the Church's relevancy and impact to the next level. Without a vibrant and effective youth ministry that helps grow adult disciples, the Church will perish.

The purpose of this book is to offer insight, encouragement, and hope to anyone in a local parish wanting to create or rebuild youth ministry. It helps equip parishes with strategies, tips, and practical tools for understanding how youth ministry is all about adult disciples apprenticing youth into discipleship. By sharing something of my story from the trenches, I want to help you articulate your parish's particular vision for youth ministry in your locale, face hurdles and obstacles with grace, plan for ongoing growth, and lead your young people as they become disciples

growing other disciples. This takes hard work, patience, and sacrifice. Some people will think you're crazy, and you might want
to quit. But you're not, and I hope you don't.

Part I

ANSWERING THE CALL

1

MAKE IT WAY MORE THAN PIZZA

Without a vision the people lose restraint;
but happy is the one who follows instruction.
—Proverbs 29:18

My middle school youth group consisted of three teenage friends: Dan, Steve, and me. We were there because our moms were heavily involved in the parish and they wanted us to be likewise involved. At the time I had no complaints. It was a great place for a middle school boy. We met on Friday nights, and most weeks we would hang out in the church gym eating pizza, downing soda, and shooting hoops. We never questioned why more people weren't there. Our youth minister was an incredible person who poured so very much of her attention into us. She would take us to the Salvation Army Thrift Store to pick up kickballs, Frisbees, and basketballs. She kept a stash of Hostess Sno Balls and Twinkies just for us. We were happy. She was our chauffeur, our babysitter, our friend—and we burned her out.

I feel bad now about some of that. In fact, I sometimes wonder if God drew me to parish youth ministry as a sort of payback. I also feel bad because our youth minister, like so many of us, tried to build momentum with teenagers in parish life only to face obstacle after obstacle. She sacrificed a great deal (including weekends when she stayed up all night with a group of teenagers) for little pay and few other tangible rewards. She had a passion for growing young disciples but no direction, support, or plans to successfully pull it off.

It's not that the parish I attended didn't care about her. Youth ministry is just one of those jobs that has a reputation for being temporary. When I started out in youth ministry, there was one question that drove me nuts: "What do you do *full-time*?" So often, I wanted to shout back, "Where do I start?" and then provide the person asking with my long list of youth ministry tasks. It's difficult to describe a job that many Catholics have never heard of and relatively few have encountered in their local parishes. These conversations were frustrating at times and at others could be quite humorous.

"So are you like a priest?"

"No."

"Are you like a teacher?"

"Well sort of. I do teach but not in a school."

"What else do you do besides pizza parties and field trips?"

"I kind of don't do that."

"So what do you do?"

"I cast vision and help teens grow in their relationship with Christ and the Catholic faith."

"Oh . . ." (awkward pause)

"Does that make sense?"

"Sure." (more awkward silence, followed by new conversation topic)

Looking back, I have a hard time blaming those curious people. I wasn't really sure at first what being a youth minister entailed, and I was one. Over time, I grew into it, learning from veterans and learning what needed to be done. It now makes sense to me and other youth ministers, but to many of our fellow Catholics, it's still a new and too-often shrouded undertaking.

So what is today's youth ministry supposed to look like? That depends on you, your church, and your community. Your youth ministry needs an identity. It needs to serve a purpose, and that starts by asking this question: "Why do *you* do youth ministry?"

CLAIM AN IDENTITY

If asked, "What's youth ministry?" would you be able to confidently respond? Would you have an answer consistent with the youth minister on the other side of your diocese? If your answer to either question is "probably not," that's a problem. If those working in youth ministry have a hard time defining it, and other people in our parishes do not know what youth ministry is, then few Catholics will care whether or not it exists.

Youth ministry as a distinct ministry in the Catholic Church is still quite new. In the early part of the last century, Bishop Bernard Sheil of Chicago started the Catholic Youth Organization (CYO). It was a ministry that sought to reach out to street kids during the difficult years of the Great Depression. In a 1955 article in *Harper's Magazine*, the CYO was described as "a well-coordinated agency meeting capably the problems of youth through child guidance, psychiatric counseling, remedial speech and reading programs, recreational activities, and group work."[1]

Slowly but surely, CYO became the center of youth activity in the American Catholic Church. Everything from dances to basketball leagues were created to bring youth to (or keep them in) church. It worked, but it didn't change much over many years, even as American culture shifted and the needs of youth grew. Because things didn't change, youth ministry or the parish CYO group became just another program vying for attention in the lives of American teens.

Today, if you look at the calendar of most youth ministers, Friday and Saturday nights are booked with event after event. While that worked in a lot of parishes eighty years ago, it doesn't work today. Teens are not event-driven; they are relationally driven. The last thing they need is another *program*.

When I took my first job as a youth minister, I saw it as a temporary position. It was something that would pay the bills and give me free time to figure out what I wanted to do with the rest of my life. When I decided that it was more than a job, my family questioned my decision. They wanted to know if I had thought it through. While they admired my decision to work for the Church, they wanted to make sure I had a backup plan or next step. They were asking, "What are you going to do next?" In other words, "What's your career going to be?" So many youth ministers leave because they don't know where they are going. They see the work they do as something to fill the time as they figure out life. It's like running on a treadmill with no fitness or weight loss goals in mind. You will likely grow bored and wear yourself out. A race with no clear end in sight is a race with no hope.

To run a successful youth ministry you need to have a picture of the end result, even if you never achieve it. Youth ministry should be focused on the development of the adolescents with whom you work into men and women, and what kind of men and women the Church calls them to become. Your ministry is meant to help and empower the next generation to grow in relationship with Christ.

The vision and mission you paint for your ministry are going to answer the questions, "Where are we going?" "How are we going to get there?" and, "Why are we doing what we do?" If you don't answer those questions, you're going to be stuck on a youth ministry treadmill. With no goals, no mile markers, and no end point, you're simply wasting the time and resources of your teens, their parents, and the parish. Whether you are a full-time employee or a volunteer, it's important to cast a vision to those you serve, as well as to yourself. Times will come when you hit obstacles, when ministry gets hard, dark, and hopeless. Knowing what you need to do and why you are doing it not only will help you but also will define you.

ARTICULATE YOUR VISION AND MISSION

A *vision statement* is a picture of what your organization or youth ministry could and should be. It answers the questions, "Where are you going?" and, "What do you hope to accomplish?" Put another way, it asks, "What is your end goal?" People involved or simply interested in your ministry want to know where you are going because it inspires them, gives them hope, and helps them to feel some sense of ownership of your efforts. As a runner, I try to picture the end of every race. Just seeing that finish line is a natural motivation. Whenever I see the finish line, my heart lightens, my pace quickens, and I push forward. Likewise, when you have a clear vision of where you're going, you, your volunteers, parents, youth, and the rest of your parish get motivated. You've given them hope and identified the finish line. You've painted a picture that's going to move them forward.

A *mission statement* answers the question, "How will you reach your end goal?" Put another way, it answers, "Why do you do what you do?" A mission statement fuels your purpose and identifies your strategy for reaching the vision you have for your ministry program. You need to know why you exist, or what you are doing can quickly become mindless toil. We tend to get most frustrated when we lose sight of our purpose.

In the movie *Forrest Gump*, the main character, Forrest, decided to go running one day for somewhat unclear reasons, and people started to follow him. Some followed just because they would follow anything that moves. Others followed because they were curious, and still others just because a lot of other people were following. Then one day, Forrest just stopped running, and a lot of people were left not knowing what to do. Much like Forrest's long run, there are going to be seasons of excitement and hype in your youth ministry when you attract a lot of people and positive attention. You will have people join your team because that's what everyone seems to be doing. It will feel great. However, if there is no clear purpose to your ministry and people do not know why they are serving or why you exist, they will leave when the excitement goes away.

Your vision and mission statements should serve as reminders of your purpose. They should be a saving grace when you lose sight of *why* you are doing what you are doing and reminders to your ministers of why they are important.

At Church of the Nativity, our youth ministry vision statement reads:

> Our youth ministry is making church matter by growing next-generation disciples who will grow other disciples, so that we can influence churches elsewhere to do the same.

Our youth ministry mission statement reads:

Love God. Love Others. Make Disciples.

FIRST STEPS

If you want a youth ministry that's about way more than pizza and has a clear vision and compelling mission, you need to do some hard work. It's not as simple as sitting down at your computer and typing out a sentence or two about what you want to do or accomplish, nor is it as simple as calling a meeting to plan a few events. It takes a good deal of time, clear focus, and persistent commitment.

1. Before all else, go to God.

Writing vision and mission statements without God is always going to lead to frustration and disappointment. Whether you are starting from scratch or adapting from previous statements, make sure you ask God to guide you, from content ideas to careful wording. This might call for time in quiet prayer, in Eucharistic adoration, and/or in fasting.

2. Align your statements with those of your parish.

Youth ministry is not meant to be a solo or stand-alone enterprise in the Church. Before you spend hours refining vision and mission statements, make sure they flow from what the pastor, and in many places the pastoral council, has set forth for the parish as a whole. As you can see, at Church of the Nativity, our youth ministry vision flows from the parish vision statement, which reads:

> Make church matter by growing disciples, growing disciples among disconnected Catholics in Northern Baltimore County while influencing churches to do the same elsewhere.

Likewise, the mission of our youth ministry is actually the same as our parish mission statement:

> Love God. Love others. Make disciples.

In youth ministry, we try to live that out with our environments, opportunities, and relationships. We focus most particularly on growing disciples who will grow other disciples. Youth ministry needs to be growing disciples in order to fuel the future of both the youth ministry and the Church. We'll revisit this concept throughout the book.

By aligning your vision and mission with the rest of the parish, you will create the capacity for intergenerational ministry. You will also allow the youth in your parish to develop a more visible, vibrant presence in the currents of parish life.

3. Know your target audience.

Who is your audience? The short answer is *teenagers*, but you need to get specific about exactly who it is that you're trying to reach. In Michael White and Tom Corcoran's book *Rebuilt: Awakening the Faithful, Reaching the Lost, and Making Church Matter*, they talk about targeting Timonium Tim. Who is Tim? "Tim is the quintessential lost person in our mission field. Tim is a good guy. If you met Tim at a party, a likely place to run into him, you'd like him. He's educated, well-dressed, and successful at what he does. Tim is married with children."[2]

As a parish, we focus on Tim because in our suburban Baltimore locale, it's through him that we will be able to reach his entire family. In youth ministry it's not as simple as reaching Tim's teenagers. While we want all of Tim's teenagers to participate in youth ministry, we mainly focus on teens at risk of becoming future Tims. These are the teenagers who are facing a world filled with relativism. They are challenged to pick a side in the science vs. religion debates. They are teens who are tempted by the easily accessible porn they discover on their electronic gadgets. They are the teenagers who are convinced that their only path to success is dictated by a college or a sport. Our Timonium Teenager is overprogrammed, highly stressed, and thirsty for something to release the pressure he or she feels intensely every day.

Our Timonium Teen also has a big heart; that's why he or she will get behind a social cause or share via social media something that has great emotional impact. Our teenager wants to do something with her life—she wants purpose and searches for it. In the end, our Timonium Teen is thirsty for a relationship with Christ; he just doesn't know it yet. We know that by targeting these would-be future Tims, we can prepare them for the day they head into the world without the safety net of home.

Get to know the lost teenagers in your neighborhood and ask yourself, "Why are they not coming to church?" As you get to know them, create a profile so you can easily identify whom you need to reach. Give them a name; it helps with growing relationships.

4. Study successful ministries.

If you are new in youth ministry or have never done this before, I strongly encourage you to look at the vision and mission of other churches. To build from scratch is so difficult, and sometimes we need a little inspiration from the words others have used. You will find this an interesting exercise and will likely be drawn to particular phrases, ideas, and meanings. If you find a vision or mission statement that you like, consider adapting it for your ministry. (It's polite to ask permission first.) If you need a place to start, you have my permission to use ours.

Not everything has to be original. In fact, since we don't live in a vacuum, nothing really can be entirely unique, but your vision and mission statements need to suit *your* situation in carefully honed language.

5. Share your statements with leadership.

Before you order all of those business cards plastered with your vision and mission statements, run them by adults involved in your ministry and other staff members. Choose individuals whom you trust to give you an honest critique. Ask them if they see the same thing as you do. Allow them to push back and share their insights. In the end, you need to make the final call on wording, but make sure you get other people's eyes on the project and consider their feedback with an open mind and close attention.

6. Give them to your youth.

On top of sharing your vision and mission with your adult leaders, you want your students' feedback as well. You are talking about them, after all. Knowing their thoughts is key. Sit down with a few teenagers you know who will tell you the honest truth and see if they understand the statements as you do. If they don't understand them, they'll never apply these statements to their lives. Then see if they get excited or motivated by the messages. Allow them to ask questions so that you can break down exactly where it is you want them to go and how you'll help them get there. Vision is not just for adults to see—young people need to see it too.

7. Write them out and tweak them.

As soon as an idea, nice phrase, or strong word comes to you, write it down. Do not dismiss a thought because you think it needs time to grow. Even if it isn't complete, write it down. Then, during the following few weeks, months, and maybe even years, revisit the statements. Tweak them so they flow and say what you feel in your heart. Above all else, make sure they're clear—not just to you, but to other stakeholders in your ministry. Don't be afraid to come back to them and hear others' feedback to review them. You know they will flow when you see them being lived out.

COMMUNICATE YOUR VISION AND MISSION

Once you've prayed, discerned, researched, and written an initial draft of a vision or mission statement, you need to make sure it becomes more than words on a piece of paper. Having vision and mission statements with no life is like running with no purpose; after a while the joy will wither and die. To make sure there is life and purpose behind what you do, you need to make sure that your volunteers, teens, and their parents know where you are going and why you exist. To communicate dynamic mission and vision statements you need to:

1. Make them concrete.

There are going to be people who have no idea what your ministry entails. Your vision statement should clear that up. A vision statement depicts a goal with a description that gives the clearest picture possible. That's why the words you use, the manner in which you craft them into sentences, and how you display or advertise the finished product are all crucial.

Keep in mind that your picture might be clear as day to most everyone who sees it, and yet it may also seem a little (or maybe very much) out of reach. If you need to break down the vision into reasonably achievable pieces or steps—and you probably do—then you should. If you've ever done a long road trip, you know what I'm talking about. If you try to drive straight through, you'll likely wear yourself out. As a parent of two small children, I know you need pit stops and stretch breaks. If the trip isn't broken into segments, the ride can feel like torture. The same can be true with creating a vision statement. You should create mile markers. Ask yourself and your advisers, "How will we know we are heading in the right direction?" According to Pastor Andy

Stanley, it's important to "clarify the win." That means building in those mile markers so everyone on the team knows what really matters. "Most churches do not have a reliable system for defining and measuring what success looks like at every level of the organization. Instead they post some general statistics that give them a vague sense of progress or failure as a church, and they go through the motions of continuing to do ministry the way they always have, productive or not. Thus it is possible for a church to become very efficient at doing ministry ineffectively."[3]

So what does winning look like in our church? How do we know what is important and what really matters?

Drawing on our parish vision statement, we know we are:

- *Making church matter* when we see teens at Mass and programs.
- *Growing disciples, who are growing other disciples* because teens are bringing their unchurched friends.
- *Influencing other churches* when we have teens invested in ministry and mission so that they can learn how to be the Church when they graduate high school.

At the end of the day, it's clear what we're looking to do. It's clear, and it can also be overwhelming when we look at the big picture. Seeing these mile markers helps us to know that we are heading in the right direction. Make sure that as you are creating your vision statement, you measure your progress, keep records, and share them.

2. Fold in inspiration.

If your vision statement says, "A place where teens learn about Jesus" and your mission statement says, "Providing teen programs," you need to go change them. Seriously. While the statements are clear, they evoke no emotion. Basically, your vision should answer the question: "Why should I care?" It's creating a picture of what could and should be. And your mission statement needs to break down the fear: "This vision is not possible." To fight that fear it should be feel simple and achievable.

Your vision and mission statements aren't just for a dedicated Christian who understands the importance of a relationship with Christ. It needs to reach the parents who are picking and choosing between investing their teen in a third lacrosse camp and your church programs. It needs to strike a chord in the teen who is looking for a place to connect to something meaningful. It needs to influence the volunteer who is giving up precious "me time" to hang out with people one-third his age.

Vision and mission statements are about not just what you do but also why everyone should care. Not everyone will, but they should present a good argument. The way you evoke emotion is linked to your wins. You need to find examples of when the vision is met. Seek out examples of how volunteers and students are living out the mission. Share those examples and fold them into the conversations you have with parents, teens, and other people you are trying to tell about your ministry.

The tendency is to look for buzzwords; in reality, these words are empty if there is no story behind them. Look for stories of life change, God sightings, anything that might help you formulate what your vision may look like. You'll know it when you find it because it just clicks. The more stories you come across, the more you will be able to craft and tweak your vision so that when people hear it and see it, they'll feel it.

3. Make them sticky.

Vision and mission statements can be clear and they can have emotion. However, if they aren't memorable, people won't embrace them. To make something stick, you need to repeat it. You need to repeat it and then repeat it again, and do it with a little creativity. That might mean using an analogy or an object so people can visually embrace the concept. It's one thing to create a vision and mission statement; it's another to communicate it. What's more, you can never overcommunicate it. In fact, if people are sick of it, that's good. It means that it's stuck.

Doug Fields, former youth pastor at Saddleback Church, shared his story in *Purpose Driven Youth Ministry* of how he used the concept of a funnel to drive home the five purposes that made up his vision statement. His use of the funnel concept became quite contagious, and his volunteers let him know it:

> Prior to coming to Saddleback Church I worked at another church for eleven years. I communicated our purpose statement with an image of a funnel. . . . Prior to one of our volunteer staff meetings, everyone secretly arrived an hour before me to create an antifunnel campaign. . . . Here was my volunteer staff whom I had been leading, nurturing, and sharing ministry with for years saying, "Enough is enough; we get the point." I felt like my leadership had been attacked.
>
> Later that night I called a mentor and shared this stinging experience. This man, who was very successful in business, said, "Doug, what they did is one of the greatest compliments I've ever heard. Most followers don't hear about purpose enough to know it, let alone get tired of it. I would be thrilled if my employees realized why our company exists. Most don't have any idea of our business outside their main responsibility. Besides, your volunteers weren't making fun of your purposes, they were having fun with your visual process. So back off on the funnels for a while, but never back off on your purposes."[4]

As his mentor pointed out, his volunteer ministers weren't mocking the vision; they were just sick of how it was being portrayed. The key is that it was memorable and people embraced it. If people know your vision and mission, they'll imitate them, live them out, and become one of the most important tools to your ministry. They'll become advocates of your mission and help it to spread and grow.

Creating a vision and mission statement is the first step, but communicating them is an entirely different one. Whether you are starting out or have been in ministry for decades, you need to consistently ask yourself, "Where does God want me to take this ministry?" and, "How does he want me to get there?"

Remember that as you build your vision and mission statements, they should align with those of your parish. If the youth ministry is heading in a different direction from the rest of the community, you'll only create conflict. Continue to craft, tweak, and continuously work on your vision and mission. You need to work at improving them, just as you might want to consistently improve a skill such as cooking or marathon running. Keep your statements concrete, emotional, and sticky. Incorporate them in whole or in part into your conversations, presentations, and correspondence. Put them on your e-mail and your website. Repeat the words, repeat them, and then repeat them some more.

Remember, a vision in God is a vision filled with his grace. A mission for God is one filled with his blessings.

2

PURSUE AUTHENTIC RELATIONSHIPS WITH SMALL GROUPS AND MENTORS

Iron is sharpened by iron; one person sharpens another.
—Proverbs 27:17

Churches can be like foreign lands for teenagers. Parents encourage their children to attend with little or no explanation of what to expect. If they walk into your church and do not see anyone they recognize, it can be horrifying. Teenagers are looking to connect with someone. If they do not feel welcomed, accepted, or loved when walking into your ministry setting for the first time, they will leave to find a place where they do.

I spent the first ten years of my life living in Japan, Hong Kong, and New Zealand. My dad frequently transferred within his company and as a result we would move to new places. I look back on those experiences with many fond memories because they brought exciting new places and cultures for me to explore. Of course, moving also meant having to make new friends. Each time we hit a new city, that process was difficult. Ironically, the most challenging time to make friends was when my family moved back to the United States. I was entering the fifth grade and I'll never forget my first day of school that year. I didn't know anyone, and while that was okay during class, it was horrifying at lunchtime. I had to figure out where I would sit. I saw two guys who I thought could be friendly. They didn't look intimidating, but boy was I wrong! After a few minutes of silence they started sharing their bloody knuckle stories. That's a game where you smack the other person's knuckles with closed fists. First one to bleed loses.

The next day I gave a different table a try. This time I found a few kids who were more my style, but I wasn't sure if they thought the same about me. I eventually opened up and shared a little bit about myself until I found a group of close friends. Over the years my relationships with them would grow and deepen. They were there for me through pivotal moments in my teenage years, and most of them are still part of my life.

One thing I learned from moving around from town to town and country to country is that being the new kid stinks. The fear of never making friends is paralyzing, and chances are that fear is a reality for some of the students in your ministry. They don't have to be new to town, but when teenagers come to your youth ministry for the first time, they're wondering, "Where should I sit?" and "Who is going to talk to me?"

If you want your ministry to grow stronger and bigger, you need to be able to meet teens where they are in life and not expect them to come to you. You need to help them feel like their presence matters and that they are a part of your church for a reason. Later on in this chapter, I will address how you can meet certain teens and take them deeper into the journey of faith, but it's important early on in this book to keep in mind that youth ministry cannot be passive. You cannot expect teens to show up and return on a regular basis because of one invitation—you'll never see results. Instead, you must pursue authentic re. which takes a good deal of time and focused effort.

When you invest in the teens of your parish, you are i.   .g them to be a part of a greater community. When they feel the investment, they begin to comprehend the value of belonging to the larger faith community. In *Renewing the Vision*, the US Catholic bishops explain this:

> If parishes are to be worthy of the loyalty and active participation of youth, they will need to become "youth-friendly" communities in which youth have a conspicuous presence in parish life. These are parish communities that value young people—welcoming them into their midst; listening to them; responding to their needs; supporting them with prayer, time, facilities, and money. These are parish communities that see young people as resources—recognizing and empowering their gifts and talents, giving them meaningful roles in leadership and ministry, and encouraging their contributions. These are parish communities that provide young people with opportunities for intergenerational relationships—developing relationships with adults who serve as role models and mentors.[1]

Basically, it's all about the relationships. If you want a thriving and growing ministry, you need to consistently look at: "Who is investing in the lives of teens in our parish (geographic area)?" "How are we investing in them?"

To help teenagers go deeper in faith and embrace a Catholic identity, you need to build intentional and authentic relationships by:

1. Welcoming them at the door.

What's their first impression? When teens walk into the building, are they greeted or does the church foster an unintentional game of hide-and-seek? At Nativity, we've created a ministry where adults (whom we call "crowd ministers") are in charge of the hospitality at each of our program events. Every week there needs to be at least one adult at the door greeting each student who walks in. The role of these crowd ministers is to first welcome a teenager and then give him or her direction on what to do next. When new students walk in and see someone waiting for them, it communicates, "I'm available to you and care about what you've faced this week." We aren't talking rocket science, just a basic habit of hospitality.

To create a welcoming environment, just find at least one adult or teen to stand at the door and welcome everyone who walks in. If the greeter doesn't know a teen's name, coach him or her to shake hands and ask for it. If he or she does know the teen, a hug or handshake is most appropriate. Have your greeters find ways to celebrate the fact that these teens are joining you, whether they are new or have been coming around for a long time. It might seem odd or even a little awkward at first; however, being intentionally greeted at the door will affirm their arrival. When people feel like they belong, they will enter with more of an open mind to what they might experience next.

2. Connecting them to one another and the wider community in small groups.

There is significant pressure for most of you to have a big, exciting, even over-the-top ministry. If that's what you want, all you need to do is create big events with professional entertainment, awesome giveaways, and lots of advertising through social media and word of mouth. If you plan these events well, you will draw large crowds. However, to sustain large numbers will be an impossible task. Consistent attendance takes an investment of time, energy, and patience. I'm not questioning your investment. I truly believe that you care about the teens in your ministry and community. However, you as one person can realistically invest deeply in only three or four of them at a time. In order to really form meaningful and deep relationships, you need to be available for each teen you pour into—that means giving him or her lots of time and attention. If you are married or wish to have any type of life outside of ministry (and you should), you cannot be personally available to all the teens in your area all the time. This is where recruiting excellent small-group leaders comes in.

I have grown convinced that every even remotely interested teen living within your parish boundaries needs to be connected to a small group that is focused on evangelization and discipleship (growing a relationship with Jesus and learning how to serve him). Through small groups, teens learn how to build Christ-centered relationships with their peers, receive wisdom from God-honoring adults, and find acceptance for who they are. In short, it is through small groups that teens are challenged and mentored on their faith journeys as they become the people God has created them to be.

At Nativity, our small groups meet on a weekly basis. Each week, teens come together in a large-group setting where they pray together and then hear a message delivered by me or a volunteer that serves as a catalyst to their small-group discussion. We give them a topic to discuss, but if something urgent comes up in a teen's life such as a breakup, troubles at home, or death of a loved one, we encourage the group to explore that situation together, with the guidance of their adult leader or mentor. Essentially, we want teens coming together to share life and pray with one another and for one another. By repeating that week in and week out, each teen develops the spiritual habit of forming accountable relationships.

We try to keep groups limited to six to eight teenagers with two to three adult leaders. This gives each teen a chance to share and to form close bonds with their peers and with adult mentors in the faith. We always pair up leaders because it brings accountability to the group. Each week, at least one of the leaders is present in each group, which leads to consistency and a supportive partnership that helps these adult volunteers walk through difficult situations. While our goal is to maintain six to eight students per group, we are okay if the group dwindles to three or four. This can be discouraging for small-group leaders, but we try to trust that God has a plan and not worry about rebuilding the numbers. Although it may not be large in size, if attendance is consistent and teens are actively engaged, the group will remain a healthy and vibrant source of formation in faith and a fertile training ground for discipleship.

Our groups are not random, and they are gender specific. Beginning in sixth grade, our students join small groups grouped by grade level. They then remain in formation with the same group through their middle and high school years. When at all possible, adult leaders also remain with the same group during those years. Yes, you read that correctly, and yes, it takes a lot of commitment and determination on everyone's part, but the outcomes are well worth the efforts.

By keeping the group consistent, walls and barriers are knocked down and tremendous trust builds. While profound conversations can happen with members of the opposite sex, they tend to go only so deep. Adolescence is a particularly fragile time in the development of self-awareness along with moral, psychological, and spiritual development, and we find that there is certain wisdom that only a man can share with a teenage guy and a woman can share with a teenage girl. If you don't have enough leaders to divide up by age, my recommendation is that you work with gender grouping first.

It's through small groups that our teens connect not only with peers but with the Body of Christ, the wider Church community. Small groups give them experience and practice in forming life-long Christlike relationships. They allow teens to see how we are not meant to travel through life alone, that God in Christ has placed us alongside one another to travel together in discipleship.

CREATE SAFE STRUCTURES FOR ONE-ON-ONE TIME

Small groups are wonderful because they promote community; however, sometimes a teenager needs focused attention. Whether it's addressing a specific life issue or going deeper into his or her spirituality, you need to be ready to provide opportunities when you and a teen can go one-on-one.

There will be a point in each teen's life when he or she doesn't feel comfortable talking to a parent about certain issues for a variety of reasons. A teen might simply feel awkward; there might be a lack of trust or fear about a parent's response. No matter the reason, teens will seek out insight and wisdom for tough situations. The crucial question of course is, "To whom will they go?" It might be a coach, a teacher, or a pastor. It might be a sibling, a classmate, or a friend. Increasingly, their first move will likely be to search for help online. As a youth minister, you need to make it a goal to place yourself or one of your well-trained volunteers near the top of that list. By creating a program structured around both small groups of peers and readily available adult mentors, you not only build trust but also provide:

    a. A God-honoring voice in their life.
    b. A resource and affirming voice for parents.
    c. A link to a personal relationship with Jesus Christ.

We encourage the idea of one-on-one connections between small-group leaders and each teenager outside of a regular gathering. When a situation arises where a teenager needs to talk to the small-group leader or a parent is struggling to communicate with his or her child, we organize a meeting. Together the small-group leader, parent, and I will arrange a time and safe location for the meeting to occur.

It's important to follow your diocesan guidelines when arranging these meetings. Before you get started, contact your child protection representative and have a constructive conversation on what these encounters can look like. The more you understand the guidelines, the more confidence you'll have in creating your program. The more you communicate with your diocese, the more they'll trust you in return.

These meetings create time and space for small-group leaders to follow up on subjects that a teen brought up in group, address an issue that a parent might not know how to approach, or explore a concern that the mentor has regarding the teen's behaviors, mood, or disposition. In any case, an adult volunteer is there to help make sure the teen is connecting with God and his or her family and continues to grow in faith.

This dual structure of small-group and one-on-one relationships is the foundation of our sacramental preparation for Confirmation, which I address in more detail in the next chapter. These relationships are key for Confirmation prep, since there is a lot of great information about the faith to be handed on during a relatively short period of time. In the end, there are many different ways to connect with teenagers. Relationships need to grow beyond the boundaries of your youth ministry and into the rest of the parish. In chapters 5 and 7, I address important intergenerational relationships that occur outside youth ministry programs. It's through these types of relationships that teens will connect, see themselves as integral to the life of the community, and commit to ongoing spiritual growth.

FIRST STEPS

You'll be hard-pressed to find anyone who disagrees with the concept that relationships are essential to a person's faith journey. Unfortunately, the largest obstacle that many of us have is finding the right adults to meet on a consistent basis with our teens—not just for a single program year but hopefully for several. As with any growth process, there are going to be pains and pitfalls. To get started:

1. Think small.

There is so much pressure to have big numbers in your ministry. The problem with thinking big right away is that you have little margin to build a structure of authentic relationships. While numbers are important to your ministry, they won't be sustainable without healthy relationships.

Think small by starting off small. Create two groups (a boys' group and a girls' group) of five to eight teenagers. Find four leaders (two men and two women) who are not only willing to lead the groups but also not afraid to make mistakes. Outsource the curriculum so that you can focus solely on the structure of the group. This means finding curriculum that works in the structure you are creating. You don't want to create a program to fit a curriculum; you want a curriculum that will fit your structure. Look for something that is adaptable. I look for content where I can use the entire package or break it up and use only certain components. A helpful resource is one where the videos, small-group questions, or activities can stand on their own.

Also look for resources that require little training or preparation for your volunteers. You want your volunteers feeling confident going into a room of teenagers. If they see something that implies they need a doctorate in theology, they might freak out. For recommendations on resources, visit my christopherwesley.org or rebuiltparish.com.

While content is important, you do not want to waste time figuring out how to use it. In fact, prioritize getting the group to meet, not the information that you will cover. Lastly, designate a limited amount of time (six to eight weeks is reasonable) during which these groups can function and grow.

At the end of the allotted time, sit down with your leaders and teens to reflect on the process. Make necessary changes and then do it again. Thereafter, build on it by increasing the number of groups and the length of time you meet. When the small groups grow, you'll be able to build around them. You can incorporate them into your large-group programs. When you think small, you'll find it easier to manage more students because the entire group is broken into smaller ones.

Thinking small is key when it comes to mission opportunities and evangelism events. Instead of coordinating a large bus, collecting dozens of permission forms, and putting the burden on yourself, you will have created a system where volunteer adult leaders are advocating for you and sharing the burden. By thinking small, you are equipping yourself to recognize the big moments and focus on the larger goals of vision and mission in your ministry.

2. Get leadership on board.

If you don't have backing, you have only so much credibility. Ideally, you want all your leaders and, most critically, your pastor and the rest of the staff on board with this idea. In many parishes, youth ministers will also need the support of the parish council. When you have support from leadership, you will be able to fund and fuel your ministry. Having leadership behind you means having powerful advocates and influence. Your pastor or pastoral life director will help you on many levels; most crucially, perhaps, they can help with identifying and recruiting potential small-group leaders.

3. Set high standards for your leaders.

When I first started in youth ministry, I was so desperate for volunteers that I looked for warm bodies who were in *any* way willing to help. Don't do that. Find men and women who are passionate not only about teenagers but also about God, the Church, and your parish's mission. Any misalignment will set you back. It will take time, often *a lot* of time, but set up a trial process in which you can determine whether or not a person is the right fit. Most employers carve out a probationary period with new hires. Don't our teens deserve as much care?

The idea of meeting with the same teenagers weekly for four or more years seems daunting. If you really believe in your ministry, ask leaders to commit for a year. To further strengthen their commitment, paint them a vision that shows the benefits of their investment. Let them know about the life changes they will see in their teens as well as themselves. If possible, find personal testimonies that speak to the power of small groups. If you can break down the journey into achievable steps, they'll see it as doable.

4. Create a basic framework.

I often hear from adults that they choose not to get involved in youth ministry because they feel underqualified. It's a valid excuse, but it's one that's easy to overcome. In addition to painting a vision for your volunteer ministers, you want to give them a framework under which they'll lead the groups. For us, it's as simple as this:

- **Pray together.** Each encounter should begin with a prayer inviting God into the conversation. It can be a simple statement or a lengthy reflection.
- **Share life.** Sharing life can be talking about what's happening in teens' lives during a game of basketball, or it can be chatting over a soft drink or doughnut between weekend Masses. Sharing life means talking, listening, and doing things that will help you get to know one another on a deeper level. If our leaders aren't creative, we give them "ice-breaking" questions to help with this.
- **Pray for one another.** Close out the experience assuring the teen that he or she is not alone. When you close your time together with sharing prayer intentions, it's a reminder that someone is thinking of and praying for you.

This framework is not only simple, but it enables the group to overcome the obstacles they will face ahead. When you pursue authentic relationships in your youth ministry, you'll discover a myriad of teenagers come to church because they understand that they are seen, welcomed, and cared for. The authentic relationships you facilitate will be the gateway for teens to form an authentic one with Jesus Christ.

3

TAKE BACK CONFIRMATION FOR MAKING DISCIPLES

Not only when I am present but all the more now when I am absent, work out your salvation with fear and trembling. For God is the one who, for his good purpose, works in you both to desire and to work.
—Philippians 2:12–13

Whether or not you have an extensive youth ministry, teenagers are still leaving the Church after they graduate high school. You can have the most dynamic youth ministry program in the world, but if that's all it is, you will be disappointed in the end. Youth ministry has to be more than engaging teenagers where they are now. It also needs to be focused on getting them ready for the years ahead. One of the greatest opportunities you have to do this is in preparation for Confirmation, assuming of course that the sacrament is celebrated during the teen years in your diocese.

I'm a neurotic traveler. It doesn't matter how prepared I am, I always feel like I'm missing or forgetting something. TSA really doesn't need to do a search on me. If you see me, it'll look like I'm giving myself a pat down constantly. I'll make sure I have my license literally a dozen times before I get in the car on the way to the airport. When I get in line for security, I have to wear a hat so that I can stuff my phone, wallet, belt, and keys in it. I triple-check my boarding pass before going through the security checkpoint, and then I check it three more times before getting in line for the plane. Although I have a smartphone, I carry physical copies of car and hotel reservations in a manila folder. I snap and scan photos of everything and store them in my Evernote, Dropbox, and iCloud accounts. What can I say? I just need to feel prepared.

Anytime you are embarking on an adventure, it's a good idea to make sure you are prepared for a reasonable number of divergent possibilities. Of course, you cannot prepare for everything, but you can set yourself up for success just in case plans need to change. It means being flexible and confident in what you do know. It requires educating yourself on what could lie ahead and what to do if things go wrong or at least not according to plan.

Church communities are called to prepare their young people to eventually set off into the world as adult disciples who will make other disciples. While there are many dynamic ways a youth ministry can prepare students, the most important step for most parishes is leading them to and through the Sacrament of Confirmation. It's through this sacrament that we echo the words of Jesus when he said in Matthew 28:19–20, "Go, therefore, and make disciples of all nations, baptizing them in the name of the Father, and of the Son, and of the holy Spirit. . . . And behold, I am with you always, until the end of the age." Unfortunately, somewhere people got the impression that Confirmation was more like Jesus saying, "Go home; you're done. No more religious education! You've graduated; here's your certificate!"

This view of Confirmation comes because we prepare for it like a graduation. We put teenagers in classes, try to fill their heads with knowledge, test them on it, and then provide a ceremony for their effort. If they struggle and we call them out on it, parents get involved and threaten to tell the pastor. Parents and teens resist the whole effort but comply because they want to get it over with and be done with religious education, or catechesis, or whatever we happen to call it. Confirmation easily becomes just another item on the checklist of good-Catholic-parent tasks and have-tos for teenagers.

At Church of the Nativity, we look at our Confirmation preparation process as a journey and situate the sacrament in our collective understanding where it properly belongs—as a sacrament of initiation. Like any successful journey, Confirmation preparation requires:

1. A Clear Path

If you were driving from Los Angeles to New York City, you would make sure you were equipped with a map or GPS, or, if you are like me, both. This would be especially true if you had never done it before. Anytime you start out on a journey, you need a plan. Some of it is given, like a beginning point and a destination. While this might be obvious for any physical journey, Church leaders so often leave out both of these factors in sacramental preparation. We usually start out assuming students are at a point in their spiritual lives and religious understanding where they are not, and we take them toward a destination that we see but they really cannot.

Before a teenager begins our Confirmation program we lay out the entire process to them and their parents. We hold an information meeting where we go over the guidelines and expectations. We ask students to apply to the program through an online application. Once they are accepted into the program, they are asked to attend a mandatory retreat over the summer. Then in the fall they begin meeting with someone we call a mentor, one-on-one throughout the formation process. This mentor is someone who guides the student through the curriculum and encourages the parents to get involved. The program then concludes in the spring with a reflection letter that serves as an "exit interview" for the process.

How you design your Confirmation program will depend to at least some extent on the guidelines provided by your diocese. If the guidelines the diocese provides are unclear to you, contact your diocesan representative and talk things over until you feel sure of what's expected. It's a good idea to loop your pastor in on this as well.

For us at Nativity, we come right out and ask our candidates to write a 500-word essay as part of their program application. The question they address in the essay is, "What type of disciple do you want to be?" It's a difficult question for most to answer, and we know that. It's a challenge because many of them have never been asked that question before. I'm not sure why; maybe it's something we ought to ask sooner, but it's an important question. Knowing what type of disciple they want to become means knowing where you need to take them. Listening carefully to how they articulate their responses should tell you something about how to get them there.

We also ask parents, "Why do you want your child to do this?" This makes the parents pause and consider whether or not the battle they might have to engage in is really worth the effort. The answers to these two questions tell us whether or not the parents and child are on the same page. Sadly, as you might suspect, that is rarely the case.

We find that teenagers are participating to please their parents, and parents are trying to meet a misaligned expectation. Many of our candidates start out in the program trying to fulfill an obligation. Our goal is to help them see it as something they get to do.

These essays help us figure out their perception and expectations of faith, the Church, and God. Before we start meeting with candidates, we want to know their perspective on discipleship. This will give us an idea of where they are in their faith journey so that we can help them figure out where it is God is going to take them. Once they are accepted into the program, we ask them a similar question that goes a little deeper. At the first meeting they have with their mentor, we ask them, "Who do you want to be in ten years?"

Too often we ask teenagers, "What do you want to do?" It's a fun question because it involves dreaming of tangible goals. Answering that question usually means knowing what college you want to attend or what job you would like to have one day. Asking, "Who do you want to be?" means searching one's soul more deeply. We ask that specific question because we want teenagers to cast a vision for themselves. We want them to start peeling back the gifts, talents, and flaws that God has planted in them and to take a good look. Before we fill them with any information, we want to help them discover what is already there.

The path you help these teens choose is paramount. You need to help them take that first step, and that means giving them a trusted guide.

2. Mentors

Before I came to Church of the Nativity, Confirmation prep was done in a small-group setting. It was effective because it allowed the teenagers to create dialogue around this enriching sacrament. However, it was still easy for a candidate to get lost in the group, to glide over a good bit of soul-searching. Once we acknowledged this, we decided to create what is now the heart of our program structure, the Confirmation mentors. These adult ministers care deeply about their Catholic faith, love the Catholic Church, and desperately want to pass that on to the youth of our parish. These mentors are men and women whom I trust and love. They are people whom I trust with my own family and who know me well. They are handpicked by me because they are a direct extension of my leadership. I link each of them with two Confirmation candidates, and they accompany the candidates through the entire preparation process.

The mentor's responsibility is to meet one-on-one with their assigned candidates and to constantly communicate with parents. When the program was first started, we assigned five candidates to one mentor. We found the workload to be exhausting and made it a goal to build up to a one-to-two ratio of mentor to candidates. This took many years, but now we're able to maintain it. If you have a large group of candidates, my recommendation is to start with small groups with a one-to-eight ratio and work toward a one-to-two ratio. Be sure to discuss a one-on-one mentoring program with your pastor and diocese. Because these adults are meeting one-on-one, you need trust, and that takes time to build.

The great thing about our mentors is how they reassure the candidates that they are not alone on the journey. Our teenagers have someone to share wisdom and the right resources—adult Christians who may be entirely new to their lives but who are entirely committed to the spiritual growth of our candidates. Our candidates choose their own sponsors, the witnesses they invite to stand with them at the celebration of the sacrament. Our hope is that after the candidate receives the sacrament, the sponsor picks up where the mentor leaves off. We communicate this while candidates are applying for the program. And then we have the mentor address it during those first couple of meetings. While there is no specified involvement during most of the preparation process, we ask sponsors to pray for their candidates. We encourage them to reach out and ask questions like, "Where are you growing?"

While it might be popular for candidates to pick an older sibling or friend, we encourage them to select an individual who will model Christ and have wisdom to help them grow. We also stress the importance of proximity. Granted, technology allows us to connect with people instantly throughout the world, but nothing beats a face-to-face encounter. We also encourage candidates to pick as a sponsor someone they see on a regular basis.

We haven't completely figured it all out, but we've seen teenagers maintain involvement in the local church when they have an adult personally investing in their faith formation both during and after the Confirmation preparation program.

3. Resources

When it comes to Confirmation, we are commissioning teenagers to go into the world and utilize the gifts of the Spirit to spread the Good News. To prepare them for the journey and to take on the grueling challenge, we need to make sure they know how to grow.

Saint Paul knew how important it was for his followers to understand how to grow on their own. In his letter to the Philippians, Paul wrote, "So then, my beloved, obedient as you have always been, not only when I am present but all the more now when I am absent, work out your salvation with fear and trembling" (Phil 2:12).

Paul knew he wasn't going to be around forever. He knew that in order for these young disciples to continue growing in their faith, they needed to know exactly what "working out your salvation with fear and trembling" meant. We should be telling this to our teenagers over and over again. It's difficult enough for them while we are in their lives. Our job, in part, is to try to ensure that they have the right spiritual habits as they move into the world.

So, what are the spiritual habits or disciplines that we should be instilling into our young people? There are so many that it can be overwhelming! At our parish, we focus on five spiritual disciplines that we call our Next STEPS (Serve, Tithe, Engage, Practice, Share). These are the steps we want every child, teenager, and adult taking. While we cover these steps in all aspects of our youth ministry, it's through Confirmation that we really drill them down.

In our large-group settings we define these steps, and in small groups we talk about what these steps look like in the lives of our friends and family. But it's in the one-on-one mentoring relationships that we get personal. It's in this setting that the mentor helps the candidate work on these disciplines independently. Through these combined efforts our teenagers learn to:

1. Serve in ministry and missions.

This step is about becoming more active in the faith community through ministry and mission. *Ministry* is serving inside the church building and campus through one of our many different volunteer opportunities. These opportunities stretch from serving with small children in our Kids' Ministry or behind a camera in our Creative Tech Ministry. We want teenagers using their gifts and talents to honor God and serve others within our parish community.

Missions refers to serving beyond our church building and campus in the local community, across the country, or in other parts of the world. Locally we have strategic partnerships with organizations that God is blessing and that are living out a similar mission. Nationally we work with organizations like Nazareth Farm and Appalachian Service Project where teenagers spend a week getting to know a community through service and prayer. We do not currently send students overseas, but we are looking to do that in correspondence with international strategic partnerships.

Our church does an excellent job providing opportunities for adults and teenagers to serve within and beyond the local church. We want our Confirmation candidates right in the thick of it, so we ask them to make a commitment to one of these ministries or mission opportunities during their preparation. It is here that we know they will not only put their faith into action but also learn to build relationships and share their faith with fellow disciples.

2. Tithe through sacrificial giving.

This can sometimes feels like an impossible task, but teaching a teenager how to tithe is giving them a gift that will keep on giving. We want our candidates tithing because it not only funds the local church but also takes them to a new level of trust with God. It's the one spiritual discipline wherein God tells us to test him:

> Bring the whole tithe
>> into the storehouse,
> That there may be food in my house.
>> Put me to the test, says the LORD of hosts,
> And see if I do not open the floodgates of heaven for you,
>> and pour down upon you blessing without measure! (Mal 3:10)

Here we adults share examples from our own lives of how God has blessed us once we've learned to be givers by way of our tithing. But before we can get teens thinking about tithing, we need to make sure they are confident with managing their money. This means explaining a budget and helping them see how they can best use their money. This takes a lot of patience and leads to interesting discussions, but if you get your teens tithing now, it will be a whole lot easier than waiting until they are adults. It's easier to give up 10 percent of $10 than it is 10 percent of $100,000. We want to raise givers.

3. Engage in small-group relationships.

Faith is personal, but it isn't private. Teens need to learn to grow with their peers. There is a lot we already covered in chapter 2 about pursuing authentic relationships; however, it's worth repeating briefly here. When teens can build accountable and faith-filled relationships with peers and adult leaders, they are more likely to succeed in their faith commitments than they are on their own.

4. Practice prayer and the sacraments.

We want the candidates to know that their most important relationship is with God. Prayer and the sacraments are excellent ways to get to know him personally and corporately. When it comes to prayer we encourage personal quiet time and scripture study and help them learn these habits.

To help teens with prayer, we introduce them to a variety of ways including devotionals, Eucharistic adoration, and journaling. Whether it's formal prayer or spontaneous conversations, we want them to get used to talking with God.

When it comes to reading and praying with scripture, we introduce them to lectio divina (divine reading). This way of meditating with scripture allows them to explore the many different layers that are found in God's Word. We also try to make the Bible accessible by showing Bible apps, teen-friendly translations, and other online resources.

By offering them opportunities to try different types of prayers, teens learn to personalize their conversations with God. This means giving them information on where they can find a perpetual adoration chapel or showing them mobile apps they can use to go deeper in their relationship with God.

When it comes to the sacraments, we want to address the fact that there are many teenagers in every ministry that do not attend Mass on any kind of a regular basis. Chances are that many, if not most, of your teens have not been to confession since their first one. I'm willing to bet many of them are not thinking about marriage, although they constantly obsess about relationships. Seeking and embracing sacramental grace is essential to our Catholic faith, yet it's one of the hardest disciplines because of the emotional baggage that might come with it.

Maybe a teen had a bad experience during his first confession. Maybe his parents are divorced. Maybe Mass has been boring for him and he checks out before consecration or skips out altogether. We try to uncover hang-ups and obstacles that prevent a teen from living out this discipline. We explain to and show our teens how to engage in sacramental life throughout our local parish, as well as the universal Church. This usually involves covering some of the basics and then literally giving them opportunities to witness or experience them.

5. Share through *invest and invite*.

Sometimes the big hurdle to evangelization is the actual word *evangelization*. First, most teenagers don't know what it means. Second, it's a word that sounds churchy and intimidating. To overcome those obstacles we break down the step of evangelization into a simple three-word strategy: *Invest and Invite*.

We want teens to find someone in their school or community who doesn't know Christ and to build a relationship with him or her. Then we encourage them to pray for an opportunity where they can share their faith or invite their friend to church. While we do not have a lot of events, we believe that our weekend Mass and student programs are environments where someone who is not Christian can feel comfortable and welcome. We walk closely with our teens through all this, helping them learn to be welcoming without being pushy, to be authentic without being overly zealous. We help them learn to spread the enthusiasm for Catholic Christianity that is growing within their own hearts and minds.

All the STEPS (Serve, Tithe, engage, Practice, Share) are reinforced throughout the fabric of our parish church. In fact you'll often find our pastor speaking about them on a weekend. They are reinforced in our small groups and crowd programs. It's in the Confirmation program where we really get personal and discuss what it is our teens need to know and what they need to do to continue to grow, even after we are gone from weekly presence in their lives.

After spending a year engaging in these spiritual disciplines, we make sure that our teens have some closure and are able to continue on in their faith journey.

4. End Zone

Our archdiocese asks that each Confirmation candidate write a letter to the vicariate bishop describing his or her journey of preparation for the sacrament. As we prepare them for writing this letter, we ask our teenagers to be honest and share with their bishop what has changed in their lives during the year of preparation. I give the candidates a copy of the essay they wrote when they first applied so that they can better see those changes. The letter isn't something new, but we treat it as a candidate's personal proclamation of faith.

When these young people reflect on their journeys, it brings a little closure. We also have them discuss their next steps during the last meeting candidates have with their mentors. We look at how they are still involved, who they've chosen as their sponsor to stand with them during the celebration of the sacrament, and what obstacles might stand in the way of achieving their goals for discipleship. The mentor is encouraged to remind the candidate that while this is the end of one leg of their lifelong journey of faith, it's not the end of a relationship. We've seen candidates long after receiving Confirmation reach out to their former mentors.

It's a sign that they still feel connected with their local church, a value we want them to embrace for the rest of their lives.

FIRST STEPS

Building or rebuilding a Confirmation program takes patience and persistence, but in most parishes it is an absolutely essential element to a disciple-making youth ministry program. It is where the proverbial rubber hits the road and where the underlying commitment to faith development for youth that will continue into adulthood becomes most apparent to large numbers of people in our parish. It will take time because you are introducing a new paradigm. People are more comfortable with what they know, and we tend to resist change as a matter of course. To bring them along and get started:

1. Identify your disciple.

List the characteristics, qualities, and habits you want your young disciples to embrace and own. Take the list and flesh it out, even if it means developing a story. Just like you would with your ministry's target audience, flesh out what a teenager who is fully committed to Christ and the Church would look like in your particular locale at this time in the history of your neighborhood.

2. Bring others into the decision.

Talk with your pastor and ask him what he expects of a mature disciple. If you have an adult faith formation director or coordinator, pick that leader's brain and collaborate on the qualities you want a disciple to possess. Sit down with the director of religious education and see what he or she is doing with younger students. Think across generational lines and various areas of church life.

3. Develop your toolbox.

After you've decided which spiritual habits you want your candidates to possess (such as the five we use), start looking at which tools will help them get there. Build a catalog of resources like devotionals, Bible studies, and service opportunities, and make these available to your candidates via adult leaders, mentors, and parents. While there are limitless options, try to narrow it down to four or five per habit.

4. Build your team.

Anytime you shift to an entirely new paradigm, find people who are committed to work through its messiness alongside you. These are people who love you, trust you, and are incredibly patient. You need to be able to trust them to own a piece of the program and so avoid control issues. When starting out, you need people helping you dream and think outside of the box.

5. Start out small.

You may feel an urgent need to switch over an entire program, but that is likely to overwhelm most everyone involved. Find a few leaders, teenagers, and their families willing to take on the challenge. After you run through an entire season of preparation, bring everyone together to gain feedback. If you are successful the first time around, repeat the essentials of the process, building on what you learned the first time through.

Confirmation is not a checklist item; it's getting your teens ready for the real world. It might feel like the biggest pain in your side. It might feel like an unsolvable puzzle, yet it has so much potential. Do not be afraid to challenge the system that's in place. If this part of youth ministry is ignored, your church will continue to produce future former Catholics. Make Confirmation relational and intentional. Make it about initiating your teens into adult discipleship with spiritual habits that will sustain their religious faith. In the end, you'll discover you are not only preparing candidates for the future but also positively influencing the parish community in which you are serving.

Part II
BUILDING A
FOUNDATION

4

CLARIFY YOUR MESSAGE

Jesus then said to those Jews who believed in him, "If you remain in my word, you will truly be my disciples, and you will know the truth, and the truth will set you free."
—John 8:31–32

We live in an age of information overload. To simply share the Gospel and the Church's teachings would only add to all the noise our teens hear on a daily basis. We assume that because we are the Church, teens will think everything we have to say is relevant to their lives. The reality is that very often what we think is clear isn't always clear to them because they are not in the right place to hear it. If you are going to grow the next generation of disciples such that they embrace the teachings of the Church and God's Word, you need to know how to deliver the message.

To explain what I mean, here's an example from my own experience. It was another frustrating night of youth ministry; nothing could make it worse, or so I thought. Then a small-group leader came up to me and asked, "Chris, can I give you some advice?" I said yes, although I was reluctant to hear any criticism just then. He continued, "I think you are doing a great job, but I think you talk for a little too long." He was right. I had their attention for the first ten minutes, and then for the next thirty they were doing anything but listening to me. While he was right, I had no desire to let him know that. I was a little embarrassed. I was also stubborn and filled with pride. He was a good guy, but I didn't want to admit that I was weak and had this wrong. So I brushed it off.

I told him, "Thanks for your insight, but I have to disagree. I think they are just a difficult group of teens." While he disagreed with me, he could sense a bruised ego. Instead of pushing back he showed me love by responding, "Yeah, I guess you're right."

I enjoy speaking, and I love sharing the Gospel. However, I haven't always been a good speaker. That was a hard reality for me to embrace, especially considering that my degree was in communications. On top of that, I had taken speech classes, I was in theater, and I had two years of youth ministry already under my belt—why wouldn't I be good? It's because catechesis is more than the transferring of information. According to the US Bishops in *Renewing the Vision: A Framework for Catholic Youth Ministry*, "The ministry of catechesis fosters growth in Catholic faith in all three dimensions—trusting (heart), knowing and believing (mind), and doing (will). The goal should be to have all Catholic youth involved in some program of catechesis."[1]

In other words, youth ministry is about growing hearts that love God and moving a generation to go and grow deeper in Christian discipleship. Too many times we throw a book at teens and say, "Memorize this." Or we talk for hours and hours about something that's important but from their view has no relevance to their lives. Moving them into deeper relationships with Jesus Christ and their Catholic faith is all about knowing what to say, when to say it, and how to say it so that they can hear. To give this next generation the wisdom they need to grow as disciples, it takes both long- and short-term planning.

LONG-TERM PLANNING

Imagine your typical ninth grade student (or sixth grader, if you are a middle school youth minister), and ask yourself, "What are the most important truths we want a teen to learn before they move on from our program?" While you might want to say, "All of them," you need to know your limits. Ideally, you'll have at least one hour each week, or about forty hours per program year, for three or four years. That means you have a total of 160 hours to share as much information as possible. While I'm sure we can think of at least 160 topics to discuss, only a few will stick.

You need to develop a plan that is going to help your teens embrace certain truths and doctrines that will foster growth in their hearts, minds, and wills. To do that, you need to remember why you exist. As a refresher, our ministry at Nativity exists to grow next-generation disciples who will grow other disciples, so that we can influence churches elsewhere to do the same. That means teaching students to do the following:

1. Love God.

It's important that teens learn why they need to have an authentic and loving relationship with God. That means teaching them ways to honor God with their time, treasures, and talents. It's showing them where these lessons or messages are addressed in the scriptures and in the *Catechism*. The more they focus on a relationship with God, the more they will see purpose in their lives. Help them embrace, in the everyday circumstances of their lives, what Jesus told his disciples at the Last Supper: "Remain in me, as I remain in you. Just as a branch cannot bear fruit on its own unless it remains on the vine, so neither can you unless you remain in me. I am the vine, you are the branches. Whoever remains in me and I in him will bear much fruit, because without me you can do nothing" (Jn 15:4–5).

The more students learn to abide in God, the more they'll feel his presence. The more they feel his presence, the more they'll be driven to go deeper.

Besides loving God teens need to learn to:

2. Love others.

Teenagers know they need to love others. The question we need to help them with is, "How do I love?" We need to show young people how Jesus wants us to treat one another. Taking them through scripture passages like the Sermon on the Mount (Mt 5–7), introducing them to traditions like Catholic social teaching, and providing mission opportunities will help drive home for them Jesus' second commandment: "Love one another. As I have loved you, so you also should love one another" (Jn 13:34).

Figuring out ways to build up authentic, accountable, and loving relationships will help your teens not only go deeper in their relationship with God but also grow enough to:

3. Make disciples.

As I said earlier, Christian faith must be personal, but not private. It's easier to teach someone how to consume religion rather than how to share faith. Youth ministry needs to convey why it's important to evangelize and give examples of how it can be done. Exploring the history of the saints or reviewing encounters Jesus had with the lost will give them tangible examples of how to share God's love. One of the best places to drive this home is through sacramental prep, like Confirmation. We'll explore that more in a future chapter.

Once you know what it is you want to teach over the long term, focus on breaking it down into manageable chunks. This is where short-term planning comes in.

SHORT-TERM PLANNING

We take an entire program year and break it down into units called message series. That means our large-group and small-group curriculum is divided up into several four-to-six-week series that go from July until May. Each series focuses on a specific subject or theme and approaches a topic that is both relevant to students' lives and essential to helping them love God, love others, and make disciples. During the message series, we'll peel that subject apart using the liturgical calendar and the *Catechism*. While having a topic is important, we still want to drill it down to something specific. That's where we want to be as intentional as possible with what we want teens to learn.

In their book *Tools for Rebuilding*, authors Michael White and Tom Corcoran asked, "Do you have a message? Prove it: Can you say it in a single sentence? In one sentence can you tell your congregation what you want them to know and what you want them to do?"[2] In other words, "What's the bottom line to your message? What is it you want them to know and do with the information you are sharing?"

For example, if we are discussing the topic of worry, we want to make sure that teens know that God is greater than all of their worries. Therefore, they can hand worries and troubles over to God with confidence in his abiding care. Over the four to six weeks of that series, we'll give them examples from scripture and the lives of others. We'll also equip them with a variety of resources. Sometimes we recommend they read a certain book or download a specific mobile app. Other times we'll do giveaways, like a postcard with a memory verse, to emphasize the bottom line.

Then, to drive the message further home, you want to make sure it's communicated in every component of your ministry. At

Nativity, we make sure that the music, small-group questions, messages, and activities parallel what we want them to know and do. The message that teenagers hear is similar to the one their parents are hearing in the homily at Mass and in their small groups. This is all a part of a collaborative initiative we call *one church one message.*

Each week our message team, composed of certain staff members, comes together to discuss upcoming message series and what we want kids, teens, and adults to know. Then each ministry crafts curriculum, small-group questions, and a message that drives home that theme and is relevant to their specific age group. By being one church one message we give families the opportunity to further the conversation beyond, "What did you learn at youth group tonight?"

FIRST STEPS

1. Drill down essential information.

Gather a team of volunteers to figure out what information you feel is essential to catechize your youth. Look again at why you exist and what you are trying to achieve. Make sure you go to your pastor, the children's director, and anyone else involved with faith formation at your church. Make it a goal to work together and embrace the one church one message strategy. That way, what you communicate can be reiterated at Mass and again at home. By drilling down the "Must-Know Truths," you'll equip your teens to continuously grow.

2. Use what you have.

The beauty of working in a Catholic parish is that you already have a framework for content. Start by looking at the liturgical calendar. The introduction to the *Lectionary* provides a useful outline to the themes of the seasons of our year. Study the *Lectionary* readings and you'll discover how they can be grouped into themes. For example, the beginning of the school year is filled with readings about creating margins and setting priorities.

The liturgical seasons such as Advent and Christmas, Lent and Easter, as well as holy days and feast days allow for various themes and topics to be explored with your teens in ways that will link what they are exploring with the rest of parish life. With this approach, not only can you drive home a specific subject but you can also introduce them to the history and liturgical life of the Church.

3. Outsource the rest.

When you start getting into the details of various elements (i.e. activities) of your program, it becomes more difficult to be original. Fortunately, you don't have to be. There is an ever-growing library of youth ministry resources available. Use these resources to help you drive home your themes and bottom lines. Instead of taking the time to make videos, create games, or develop small-group curriculum, you can use prepackaged material instead. This will create more capacity to focus on leader development.

If you are not sure where to start, a few websites I recommend are Download Youth Ministry (downloadyouthministry.com), Project YM (projectym.com), and Youth Ministry 360 (youthministry360.com). Don't be afraid to just search for *youth ministry games* online. Granted, some of them take a little bit of financial investment, but in the end it will be worth it.

4. Evaluate and analyze.

Truth will never change, but the world around you will. Do not settle for the same stump speech or core curriculum each year. Take time to analyze the effectiveness of what you are sharing in your messages. Look at adjusting examples and media you use.

Do not be afraid to sit down with your volunteer team, a group of parents, or teens to stay current on what exactly needs to be shared.

When you give the next generation wisdom that never fails, you prepare them for the battle of everyday life. By helping them discover what's relevant and what's important, you will find them returning the investment. When you inspire the mind, the heart, and the will of young people, you create a movement that will inspire your entire church community to go and grow deeper.

5

SHAPE A DYNAMIC TEAM

If the one falls, the other will help the fallen one.
But woe to the solitary person! If that one should fall,
there is no other to help.
—Ecclesiastes 4:10

One common reason youth ministers do not last is a lack of a support. The pastor might be supportive and the teens might be fans, but if a youth minister isn't surrounded by a dynamic team, he or she will struggle. Youth ministry is not to be done alone. Jesus did not travel alone; he gathered a group of disciples who believed in his mission and were able to expand his reach. Follow in his footsteps—gather a group of volunteers to help you succeed.

I remember debating whether or not to include the question (director toward parents), "Would you like to volunteer?" on our middle school program application. I thought it was a waste of space because I would get few, if any, responses. I wondered, "Why would parents want to help me? After all, aren't I supposed to be helping them?"

In the end, though, there it was, a little check mark in the yes box. I felt like Charlie in the film *Charlie and the Chocolate Factory* as he peeled back the wrapper to discover the final golden ticket. It's funny because it wasn't like this was my only volunteer, but it was the first one I recruited on my own. I jumped on my computer, opened my e-mail, and shot a "Thank you for making my day" e-mail to Jeanette. Little did I know that God had blessed me with someone who would not only help me welcome teens but also grow the youth ministry to where it is today.

It's amazing the many different ways God has blessed me with volunteers. They've come through announcements from the pulpit, invitations from friends, and simple curiosity about what we do for our teens. I wish I could say, "Here's the magic word for successfully recruiting volunteers," but it's taken a lot of work. I would love to tell you that everyone who has joined is still around, but lives happen and people move on. I would love to tell you that everyone who has been a part of my team has been an extraordinary example of Christ, but sometimes you have to learn in the most difficult ways just to let go.

Building a dynamic team of volunteers is difficult. Many youth ministers get into ministry because they want to influence young people's lives. If you want to make that impact—great! It means going beyond your own capacity. That takes work and a readjustment of how you approach youth ministry. While managing a team of people who volunteer their time is a challenge, it is nowhere near as difficult as going at youth ministry alone.

You might be the most qualified person for the job, but that doesn't mean you should be leading alone. In fact, by building your team, you can increase your capacity to reach more teenagers. Any ministry done alone is one filled with pride and fear. If you cannot share the burden and responsibility, your ministry will fizzle out.

FOCUS ON HEALTH

Getting people on board is not as simple as just shooting out an invitation to volunteer. You need to make sure you are ready for people to serve. This means having systems and structures in place that promote growth in their personal discipleship, not just use the generous gift of their time and energy. To reduce turnover and build a healthy ministry team, try the following:

1. Create a structure for reporting.

Once you get things going and your team begins to grow, it's going to be more and more challenging for you to manage everyone. Look to create a system of "leaders of leaders." Ask people you trust, who have served alongside you for a season or two, to mentor and train new volunteers. Create a shadowing program; it will give others in your ministry ownership of the vision and program. Everything will become less about you and more about a team as you add tiers of accountability and reporting. While you might be in charge, you have others to help you cast vision, train others, and build support.

2. Supply resources and training.

Anything you have used to grow as a youth leader needs to be shared with the men and women who serve alongside you. Books, podcasts, webinars, and conferences are all beneficial to your volunteers. Give it away, bring them along, and just share what you know. The more they grow as individuals, the more confident they will be when it comes to investing in your teens.

3. Hold high standards.

In order to create a quality ministry, you need quality volunteers. Many of us have at some point simply settled for anyone who was willing and available. All that does is lead to many awkward and unfortunate situations. While you want to make ministry accessible, you also need to make sure you abide by your diocesan child protection guidelines. You might be tempted to compare your diocesan process to another's and think he or she has it easier. All that will do is cause frustration in you, and that will slow you down from recruiting the right people. Embrace the policy and see it as an opportunity to get the right people on board.

Take your leaders through a list of expectations, including the child protection policy, your values, and goals. Have them sign a contract or covenant showing that they are on board. If you feel like anyone is violating the opportunity you are giving them, lean in to the situation. Do not be afraid to let someone go if he or she is holding the ministry back. Sometimes you need to fire a volunteer, and it's good to face that as you set about shaping your team. If you want to take your youth ministry to the next level, you need people you can trust, confront with any problems that arise, and challenge as they work alongside you.

4. Invest in them personally.

You won't be able to do this for all of your volunteers, and that's okay. I know my limitations have prevented me from pouring into people in the past; therefore, I've missed out on some big opportunities. Your volunteers are people with real jobs and families. When you take the time to get to know them and what they do, you build a strong bond. Not only will you find men and women to help you grow your ministry, but you'll also find people willing to help you grow as a person, just as you will help them do the same.

WHEN IT DOESN'T WORK OUT

I never saw it coming. Actually, I didn't want to see it coming. It was a situation that should have been addressed months earlier, but I was consumed with excuses for not leaning in. I finally came to terms with the situation when one of my volunteers e-mailed me to say that she was quitting because of it. She was leaving because she could no longer work with the volunteer I had placed in leadership. She was not the only one who felt that way, and tensions in the ministry were high.

The truth was that this volunteer was in over her head. I had given her a good deal of responsibility and she was not handling it well. It was a tough spot because she had been loyal, faithful, and dedicated for many years, but she had hit her limit. When things got difficult, she should have come to me. When I noticed she was struggling, I should have gone to her. Neither of us acted, and the problem escalated. Eventually she took her frustration out on others.

I called her into my office with sadness and fear. I had never really fired a volunteer before. As I explained the situation and my decision to her, she graciously accepted, much to my relief. I would like to say that was the toughest moment I had letting go of a volunteer, but that would be far from true.

Volunteers aren't a permanent part of your ministry. Just as the church will grow and evolve, so will your youth ministry. That means seeing people come and seeing people go. No one likes to let go of volunteers, but it's often necessary. If you do not help them move on, you will harm the health of your ministry. Instead of having people who are joyfully serving, you'll have a few individuals making everyone miserable. To avoid these difficult situations, it's important to do the following:

1. Lean in to conflict early.

A few years ago I noticed a volunteer showing up late on a regular basis and canceling a few times. Instead of ignoring the problem like I did in the previous story, I approached the volunteer and asked, "How are things going?" The volunteer sighed as if I had lifted weights off of his shoulders. This person started to share with me a busy schedule and some tension at home. I didn't want to lose the volunteer but knew he needed to take some time away. We agreed to give him three weeks to just reflect and pray.

Three weeks later the volunteer came in and told me that he needed to step down. We prayed on the decision and I wished him well. I was sad with the decision; however, the relationship I had with him stayed strong. Two years later he stepped back into ministry.

Anytime you feel a little tension, investigate it. If you are unsure how to handle it, take time to sit with someone to develop a plan. Never approach conflict on your own. Consult others by seeking their advice. Spend time in prayer and ask God for strength. There might be pain at first, but it will be nothing compared to what you're likely to face if you let the problem simmer.

2. Partner up.

If you hit a situation (and you will) where someone needs to go before he or she is ready, make sure you are not alone. When you go in alone to confront someone and ask him or her to step down, it can get awkward, even painful, quickly. A lot of emotions can emerge, leaving the door open for confusion. Have someone sit in with you who can objectively hold you both accountable. If you are meeting with someone of the opposite sex, be sure that another team member is there as well. Going in with someone to dismiss a volunteer protects you from any miscommunication and often helps ease hard feelings.

3. Recognize that ministry has seasons.

Whether it's at the end of the summer, the school year, or the calendar year, you need to check in with your volunteers. You can send out an e-mail or invite them in for one-on-one conversations. Review the covenant that you had them sign and ask how they are feeling about the ministry. Give them the opportunity to share where they are in their personal faith journey. Take the opportunity to determine whether or not they are burned out or feeling called to something else. This way you can approach what may become difficult situations with less tension and together come up with a variety of helpful solutions. If someone needs it, you can give that person some time away from ministry or help him or her find a better fit. Although his or her service may stop, a positive relationship between the two of you can continue.

4. Help them to move on.

Everyone has limits when it comes to serving in ministry. You want to avoid hitting those limits unprepared. You may feel like it's time for some volunteers to move on, but they may not agree. They may not be sure what the next step is and therefore feel trapped. Help leaders move on by addressing the possibility early and letting them know their options.

If someone serves as a small-group leader for four years, the last thing we want him or her to do is commit to another four years right away. We ask volunteers like this to look at a different ministry within the church or within our youth program. If they stay in youth ministry, we ask them to do something that will provide space and time to reflect on the previous four years. You want their youth ministry experience to end on a high note, recognizing it as a spiritual experience. Giving them time to reflect is like offering them a sabbatical.

Nick and Tina walked into the high school ministry early on in my tenure. I'm confident in saying they had no idea what they were signing up to do. Fortunately, they stuck it out and helped it grow. They became not only some of my strongest leaders but also my closest friends. There were times I could count on them to fill holes in my leadership. They supported me through rough nights when no one was showing up. They persevered by my side, and I'll always profoundly appreciate the role they came to play.

After five years of serving, Nick approached me about moving on. He said that both he and Tina were curious about their options, but they weren't ready to tackle them yet. I told Nick that they had earned a spot anywhere in the ministry. However, before they actually left, they had to help me replace them. Over the next year and a half, Nick and Tina helped me build a strong team so that when they left, the program would continue to grow. I miss seeing them on Thursday nights, but I'm so excited to have them in their new roles as Confirmation mentors.

FIRST STEPS

If you are coming into an already established youth ministry, you will likely inherit a few volunteers from the last administration. In chapter 9, I offer some hints about what to do with them. Chances are that some will move on. Even if all of them stay, your ministry will grow and you will need to know how to build your team. While there is no silver bullet, there are simple steps you can take to start getting people involved:

1. Invite.

Make a simple invitation over and over again. Whether it's a pulpit announcement, a spot in your bulletin, or simply an e-mail blast, the best way to recruit volunteers is through an invitation.

Granted, you need to prepare yourself to hear no as a response, and that's okay. Rejection is normal and to overcome it you need patience and persistence. No matter what you do, don't stop inviting people to serve.

2. Welcome.

The idea of serving in student ministry can be daunting for adults. You are asking them to make an investment into someone's life. To help them ease into the grind of youth ministry, create entry-level positions. For us, that's opening the door or selling pizza. All someone needs is a friendly smile and the courage to say hello. As volunteers become more comfortable, give them a little more responsibility. Ask them to lead the prayer, create an activity, or come in early to help you set up. In short, make the ministry welcoming by making it accessible.

To make youth ministry more accessible, be clear with what you want volunteers to do when they arrive. Make sure any materials they need are available, and check in with them so that if they have questions you can clear them up. The more accessible your ministry, the more confident adults will be.

3. Cast vision.

If you want volunteers to be in it for the long haul, you need to help them see the big picture. Understanding your ministry's vision will help them overcome any questions about commitment. It will help them take ownership of the ministry because they'll know why their role is so important.

4. Assess their experience.

As your ministry grows, it's important to check in with your volunteers to learn what they see. We like to assemble some of the newer volunteers to share their opinions. By doing this, we get a fresh perspective on what's going on. When you are in the trenches of youth ministry for years, it's easy to take things for granted. New volunteers will help you see some of the problems you might have been shoving to the side.

We also started sending out a survey to our volunteers. This survey doesn't evaluate only the program; it evaluates leadership. This can be humbling, but it's worth it. Giving your team permission to evaluate you builds trust and accountability. Not all the answers will be 100 percent honest, but it will give you insight into how they experience your leadership.

5. Create a culture.

Make your ministry the best one to serve in. Create a culture that your volunteers will want to tell their friends about. Tell them over and over again, "If you know someone you think would be great in youth ministry, let me know." They have people in their lives whom you are not aware of, which means your capacity to recruit has expanded. They'll know of neighbors, spouses, friends, and family members who can come in and contribute. Share the burden of growing your team with other volunteers.

Some of my closest friends are people who have volunteered in student ministry at Church of the Nativity. I remember Doug Fields (author of *Purpose Driven Youth Ministry*) telling me and a group of other youth ministers that if he were to walk into a restaurant and see one table filled with teens from his ministry, one filled with parents, and another filled with his volunteers, he would go sit with the volunteers. He explained that when you serve in the trenches of ministry with other people, you build a tight relationship. It's like going into battle together when you take on what's happening in the lives of so many young people.

I love the men and women who serve alongside me. I wish I could show them how much. I wish I could tell you each and every one of their stories. There have been times when I wanted to quit, but they picked me up. There have been times when they've connected with teenagers and their families in ways I could never imagine. They've served not only the youth ministry at my parish but my family as well. I have an incredible group of men and women serving alongside me, and I thank God for them every day. They are the best. My hope and prayer are that you can find people just like them in the ways that matter most.

6

MAKE IT IRRESISTIBLE

God looked at everything he had made,
and found it very good.
—Genesis 1:31

If your church isn't seriously investing in its youth, chances are you struggle finding a place to meet. Every week is like the TV show *Extreme Makeover* as you take the boiler room or nursery and make it a place where teens want to hang out for an hour. If you are serious about helping teens grow and go deeper in their relationship with Christ, you need an environment that's an enhancement, not a distraction.

In my senior year of college, I lived with my roommates in an old Victorian house. It had character and history, and was perfect for seven college-aged guys. Each of us had our own broken-in space. We loved that house, yet how we treated it told a different story. There were times we rode laundry baskets like sleds down the steps. There would be weekends when we would lock ourselves away, flip over couches, turn out the lights, and play capture the flag with Nerf guns. Mice were our friends and mold was no stranger. I'm not sure what our parents, friends, or girlfriends thought when they walked into the house, but to us it was home.

Today as a homeowner, I take a little more pride (well, actually a lot) in where I live. If I had any of the habits I did as a college student, I'm sure my wife would have left me long ago. A lot of the positive habits I have today are because of my wife's love of a clean house. In fact, the only time the house's cleanliness becomes a problem is when she is out of town. Even when close, dear friends who know the imperfections of our lives come over, she wants to make sure they are walking into an irresistible, welcoming, and loving environment. My wife is not overly meticulous; she just understands the value of a clean house. When your house is clean, people are comfortable and you're being hospitable.

KEEP IT WELCOMING

Having quality space is a value we can all understand. If you visited a restaurant that was dirty, chances are you wouldn't go back. If you walked into a dirty movie theater, would you really want to sit down? When it comes to youth ministry, though, it seems to be the opposite. In too many places, the youth room is an afterthought, or at least appears to be. Maybe most people assume teens won't notice or care how their space looks, but this isn't the case.

Does this sound familiar? Somewhere in the bowels of the church basement or in a corner of an old convent lies your youth room. It's furnished with mismatched couches and coffee tables your grandmother didn't want anymore. You try to personalize it by having the teenagers cover the walls with graffiti, but there is no amount of paint that can hide the fact that your space needs an upgrade.

I'm not sure what your ideal space looks like. Maybe it's got a foosball or Ping-Pong table. Maybe there are giant screens, with big beanbag chairs and trendy furniture. When you think of your ideal space, you think of a setup and layout and you tell yourself the only thing holding you back is a tight budget. Sometimes it isn't about filling your space with new stuff as much as it is about maintaining and keeping clean what you already have. As mentioned before, if your space isn't clean, people aren't comfortable. Wouldn't it be a shame if someone left your ministry because she wasn't sure about the stain she was sitting on?

Keeping the student space clean is important yet time-consuming. After a long night of energy-sucking ministry, the last thing you want to do is clean the cheese puffs and peanut butter out of the carpet. You might have people say, "Hey, can I help you clean that up?" but you are so tired you just say, "I'll take care of it tomorrow." Then tomorrow comes, and the next day, and the next day, and the next thing you know it's twenty minutes before the program starts up again and your youth space is a mess. Although we tell others not to judge a book by its cover, the teens, their parents, and even your ministry volunteers will judge your room negatively if it is not clean. If you want your ministry to be held in an irresistible environment, the first and most affordable step is keeping it clean. A messy youth minister is a disorganized youth minister, so keep your space clean.

BE INTENTIONAL

When you create an irresistible environment, you create a space that is inviting, warm, and welcoming. When the students in your ministry feel that way, they will open up. While cleanliness is an important part of the equation, there is a whole lot more that goes into creating the best space possible. Along with a clean space you need to look at the following:

1. Furniture

Yes, it needs to be in good shape; however, what you pick is important as well. We stress that our youth ministry is not a religious education class; it's all about personal relationships. To help drive home this point, we set up our space to feel like a family room. This was not an easy concept to attain.

When I first started, we had all the middle school students sit on the floor. However, I began to notice that during our talks and reflections they grew restless. I thought to myself, "We need structure." I set up chairs in rows, which worked. The students now faced me; however, while I spoke, I noticed a certain clanking sound. The chairs were metal and the students decided to move around in them, so when I spoke I would hear, "Clank, clank." They didn't care that I was revealing to them profound truth. They didn't care that I was pouring into their lives; they were uncomfortable, and they were amused by the "Clank, clank." It was horrible. To this day, I can't help but get shivers every time I pass a metal folding chair.

We got rid of the metal chairs and invested in couches and giant beanbag chairs. The beauty of the giant beanbag chair is that children will sink into it to the point where they are trapped by its soft—and quiet—cushiness. While no setup is perfect, this adjustment has done wonders for us.

In our small-group rooms we used to have the teens sit around tables (again in the metal chairs), but we found that this was too much like school. Teens had more fun writing on the tables and kicking the teen beside them, so we did away with them as quickly as possible. Now teens sit on couches that are set up in a square. Everyone, including the small-group leaders, sits on them.

I realize furniture can be expensive, but it has such a high value in your ministry. My suggestion is to make a wish list and each year budget at least one or two new items. Look out for sales and share your desires with the pastor or anyone else who can assist. In the meantime, be creative and try different things. In the long run, an investment in your furniture will pay good dividends.

2. Lighting

Fluorescent lights give me headaches. I need natural lights or incandescent bulbs in order for my mind to focus. I know people who like it bright and others who want a room dimly lit. People have lighting preferences. That means lighting in your youth room is essential because it affects how your teens participate in your program. If it's too dark, they can't read any materials; they might fall asleep and you risk the distractions you can't see (like clank, clank). If it's too bright, they'll be distracted by all the crazy stuff in your room. Depending on your program's setup, if you can control the lighting for different components, you'll be in a good place.

For our worship setting we turn off the house lights (fluorescent) and line the room with lamps. On our stage we have spotlights that are controlled by a tech team of adults and students. Lighting is about creating a mood and focusing attention on a person or object.

When it comes to small-group space, it's important for us to give it that living-room feel. It's in a living-room setting where people open up. Too many times we see youth spaces mimic classrooms, which are too formal. The space needs to be inviting, and the right light will convey that. We'll have a few overhead lights on with a couple of lamps. Students who can see properly are students who will engage in conversation and activity more easily.

Like furniture, lighting and other technology can be expensive. Again, be creative, build a wish list, and try different things out. In the end it will be worth it because you will have a group of fully engaged teenagers.

3. Temperature

Now that you've gotten this far into the book, I think I can get a little personal with you. I sweat a lot. There is nothing more unseemly than trying to watch someone with huge sweat stains under his armpits, and unfortunately that can be me. On top of my own body temperature reaching unruly limits, if it's too hot, the stench of middle school teens who have not yet learned the importance of deodorant will create a most unpleasant space. Room temperature will also affect the attention of your crowd. Temperatures too hot can lead to drowsiness, but too cold can mean excessive movement. If I had to pick, I would rather have the room too cold than too hot. You shouldn't have to choose. Make sure the thermostat is working and try to keep it between sixty-eight and seventy-two degrees. The building's temperature may be out of your control, so talk with the building supervisor or you will risk an assault on your sense of smell and the audience's attention.

4. Sound

Quality sound means quality communication. If you turn on the radio and hear static, chances are you will switch stations. If there are distractions when you communicate, people will switch you off. If you speak to a large group, it is essential to use a microphone. It allows you to speak in a normal tone, and when you sound conversational, people will engage. When people refuse a microphone they sound strained and unnatural. If a microphone is unavailable, then look at the setup of the room, change around the seating, get closer to your audience, and *practice*. Again, you don't want to sound like you are yelling or screaming. In the end, it's about sounding as natural as possible. If people are too focused on how different you sound instead of what you are trying to communicate, you'll lose them.

Besides basic communication, sound can set the mood of your environment. However, when using it to set the mood, make sure it doesn't distract from what you want to do. I was once leading a reflection where I carefully selected a playlist for background music. Afterward, a leader came up to me and said, "Chris, good job; however, I need to know who those musicians are. I couldn't help but listen to the music while you were speaking." Background sound can enhance the experience, but it can also be a distraction.

It's best to experiment with different settings. You shouldn't be afraid of silence. Having a quiet room might seem awkward, but it can also enhance the experience. Our teens live in a world filled with so much noise that having them sit in silence will create a tension they've rarely felt. It just might force them to listen to their own hearts and, with that, the voice of the Holy Spirit.

FIRST STEPS

1. Dream of your ideal space.

If someone walked into your ministry with a blank check to build your own space, would you know what to do with it? Many of us forget to dream big because we'll take anything that's available. Instead of creating programs that react to the space, think about creating space that will react to the program. When you dream about your ideal youth space, you'll find yourself approaching youth ministry differently.

2. Make it a budget item.

Not many people have the finances to do a complete home make-over. They'll save and plan to create a home that is ideal for their family situation. Youth ministers need to start allocating a piece of their budget toward environmental needs. One year it might be a giant beanbag, and the following year you may put your money toward a brand-new microphone.

Your budget might be limited—that's why it's important for you to talk to your pastor and parish bookkeeper. Do the research on every item you hope to purchase and make sure you can explain clearly why it's important to have. Part of the key to building an irresistible environment is by investing in it intentionally.

3. Learn to share what you have.

You might find yourself in the situation where you share space with another program (or several programs). This can be a difficult situation, and that is why you need to make sure you consistently communicate with everyone who is using the space.

To successfully share space with another program:

- **Respect other people's property.** If they bought the new television for their program, ask before using it. If you make a mess on their furniture, clean it up. You respect them and they'll respect you.
- **Normalize after use.** In college, I took a few film courses and at the door of the studio was a sign that read: Be Sure to Normalize. The sign was obnoxious; however, it kept us accountable. Rarely did you find equipment lying out in the middle of the floor. This allowed us to spend more time filming and less time cleaning. Clean up your messes and return the area back to a neutral setting. This way nothing is lost, the space is kept clean, and you can spend more time on ministry.
- **Learn to compromise.** You are going to have to say no to certain ideas for your space. I tried having an air hockey table for our programs. It was a huge success, but it created significant problems because there was no place to store it. Eventually we had to get rid of it.

By focusing on each component of your environment, you will create not only an engaging environment but also one that your teens will consider a second home. While money might help you enhance the experience, there are small adjustments that you can make to the overall comfort of your space without needing to break the bank. In the end, though, remember that environment is only a piece of the puzzle. If you aren't creating consistent opportunities and authentic relationships, your teens will lose interest and walk away.

While you think about how you are going to create the opportunities, relationships, and environments your ministry needs to thrive, understand this doesn't all happen overnight. It takes seasons of tweaking and adjustments. It takes insight, wisdom, and research, and you are never done. If you want your ministry to grow, you need to constantly check in and make sure you are growing healthy.

7

GO BEYOND THE YOUTH ROOM

But you will receive power when the holy Spirit
comes upon you, and you will be my witnesses
in Jerusalem, throughout Judea and Samaria,
and to the ends of the earth.
—Acts 1:8

Just because your church has a youth ministry doesn't mean that most members know what it does. This is a pretty sobering reality to a lot of youth ministers. It's the reason we struggle to get support and volunteers. If you want your youth ministry to grow, you are going to have to know how to go beyond the youth room.

"Mr. Ross saw you on ESPN again this weekend." I wasn't sure if my mom was happy about it or not. I was secretary for the student fan association X-treme Fans at Xavier University. One of my responsibilities was to show that Xavier University had some of the most die-hard fans in college basketball. To help this cause, fellow board members and I would paint our entire bodies blue and scream at every home game. If you ever watched a Xavier home game at the turn of the twenty-first century, chances are you saw me, or a blue version of me.

We knew we would never gain the prominence of Duke's Cameron Crazies, but we were hoping to get at least some recognition. The goal of our club was to bring fan support to not only men's basketball but also to other sports like baseball and soccer. To promote the other sports, we would host pep rallies and giveaways. Once we bought 200 burritos from Chipotle for a men's soccer game. I went home that night with 175 leftover burritos. It was a struggle, but we enjoyed advocating for all the sports at Xavier.

The teens in your community are craving to connect with someone worth following. Your programs can have great relationships within it, but they really need to go beyond the youth room. The entire church should strive to be intergenerational because it will give it new life. Your parish's greatest obstacle to investing in its youth is a lack of advocacy for teens.

At first you will be limited in your advocacy, especially if you are new. If this is the case, there is one person you need to rely on to help you get the word out. That person, the one who must have your back and be willing to advocate on your behalf, is the pastor.

THE PASTOR

The pastor can be your biggest advocate (even bigger than you) when it comes to youth ministry, but the only way he can help you is if you help him understand just why youth ministry is essential to the life of your parish. Help him see the reasons. That means:

1. Make your relationship with him a priority.

If you and your pastor cannot work together, you might need to consider a different place of employment. As long as he is in charge, you need to support, honor, and respect him. If you can't, it's unfair to you, the church, and your pastor for you to keep trying to make your job work.

Keep the communication flowing and get to know one another personally. Do not be afraid to confront him—privately. Embrace his leadership and constantly ask him, "How can I serve you?" When your pastor sees your loyalty and trusts you, then he will go to bat for you.

2. Let him in on the details.

One of the best things you can do for your pastor is to prepare him so that he is never surprised. If something goes wrong in your ministry, it's best that he finds out from you first instead of from someone else. Letting your pastor in on the details keeps the communication open, whether it's good or bad news.

I meet weekly with our pastor about the day-to-day operations of youth ministry. Some of it's important to what he's doing and affects the decisions that he makes as a pastor. Some of it is just letting him in on the wonderful things happening in youth ministry. If someone comes to him about the student ministry, he can confidently answer for me. The more he knows about your ministry, the more likely he will share it with others.

3. Share what you know.

The resources related to youth ministry and adolescence are constantly growing and changing. Even as a full-time youth minister, I have a difficult time keeping up. The reason your pastor might not seem interested in youth ministry is because it can be difficult to keep up with what's current. He's got a million things on his mind, so give him a little grace and feed him with what he absolutely should know.

For us, that's talking about social media, popular trends, and what's grabbing the attention of our youth. I also like to share with him books I'm reading, people I'm following, and resources

I use to keep up with the culture. If you can, bring him to a youth ministry conference. Your goal is to make sure he's never wondering, "What am I paying this person to do?" Whenever your job is a mystery, it can create suspicion in the relationship. Keep him in the know and he'll approach youth ministry with more confidence.

4. Empower him to connect with youth.

Your pastor has a platform that can accelerate the growth of your ministry. I'm blessed that my pastor allows me to share that platform. Each week, I have the opportunity to address the congregation through a variety of announcements (which aren't always about youth ministry). It allows the members of our church to put a face with my name. It is also a way for him to say to everyone, "This guy is worth my time and should be worth yours."

Your pastor can also connect with the youth in how he speaks. I'm not saying he should learn the lingo of teenagers, but you certainly can encourage your pastor to acknowledg their presence through the homily. When using analogies or examples, make sure he asks himself, "How will a young person hear this?" Make sure he doesn't come across as patronizing when he communicates directly with teens. Encourage him to be authentic but also aware that everything he has to say might not connect with them. If the teenagers feel like the pastor is speaking to them without patronizing them, they'll listen. They'll see that the church community cares that they are present. When they see the pastor investing in them, they are likely to invest back.

MINISTRY AND MISSION

When I was growing up, the teens in my home parish had limited roles in the fabric of the church. You could be an altar server, but that was pretty much it. It's not that teens weren't allowed to usher, read, or sing—they were just never asked. I often wondered how anyone got involved. It just seemed like people appeared in various roles. There was never an announcement from the pulpit or an invitation in the bulletin. I admit I had no clue how someone got started with being a Eucharistic minister, usher, or children's catechist. It was pretty much a mystery. Maybe there was some secret adult code to keep the teenagers away.

Again, service through ministry and mission are important discipleship steps for the people in our parish. They help us love others, honor God, and grow disciples. At Church of the Nativity, ministry and mission are a large part of why our weekend matters. If you walk into our building on any given Sunday, you'll not only see hundreds of adults serving in a variety of capacities, but teens serving right by their side. It's one of the best ways we encourage intergenerational ministry. Teens are opening doors, serving coffee, playing music, and caring for small children. Teens are welcomed to serve in almost any capacity, even in leadership roles.

Too many times we put teenagers in roles where there is no interaction with adults. If they have no one to apprentice them, they are missing out on an essential part of their spiritual growth. Service and volunteer opportunities in your parish need to include teens and adults. The United States Conference of Catholic Bishops states the importance of intergenerational relationships when they say, "intergenerational relationships provide young people with rich resources to learn the story of the Catholic faith experientially and to develop a sense of belonging to the Church."[1]

While you can have effective life sharing among peers, there is something more that you can get from intergenerational relationships. Teens will experience huge growth every time an adult pours wisdom into their lives. You need to figure out different ways adults can do that.

To build intergenerational ministry through service and volunteer opportunities, you need to make sure of the following:

1. It's clear and accessible.

It's easy to say, "Teens don't care about church because they are not at all involved." The truth is they might not know how to get in. Make sure you are consistently putting out an invitation. Let them know how they can sign up and whom to contact for further information. Clarify the steps they need to take. If needed, follow up and be available to walk them through the process.

2. It's equipped with teen-loving adults.

Do not send teens to a place where they will not be supported. Better yet, do not create a service opportunity where teens are not welcomed. If possible, find adults who would be willing to personally mentor a teenager ready to serve in the church. Allow them to shadow an adult who will show them the ropes and invest in them personally as they grow. Create an apprenticeship of how to be the Church through your service opportunities.

3. You hold high standards.

Treat teens like they are adults and watch them exceed your expectations. The temptation is to patronize teens because we are afraid of making things too complicated. Unfortunately, if you make them too simple a teen might not value the experience. Raise the bar, set expectations, and treat your volunteers like they are employees. Teens will thrive when they see you expect a lot from them.

FIRST STEPS

1. Develop a presence.

Does your parish know you, as a person, exist? I know that might be an odd question, but there was a time when people didn't know I was employed by my church and what I actually did on a day-to-day basis. Lay ministry is relatively new to the Catholic Church and many Catholics still don't expect full-time employees outside of the pastor, other priests, a maintenance man, and a secretary. If your parish doesn't know that you exist, then they'll be able to learn only so much about the youth ministry. As the youth minister, you are the face, the spokesperson, and the advocate for the youth of your parish. Shake a lot of hands and make sure people know you.

You might push back on this and say, "I like being behind the scenes" or, "It's supposed to be about Jesus." Yes, you might prefer not being in the spotlight, and yes, it does need to be about Jesus, but that's not going to happen if no one knows that's what you are striving to do. You cannot grow disciples if people do not know you are there to grow disciples. Be sure to:

2. Connect on the weekends.

The next two comments might be hard to digest, but trust me on this:

- Sundays should be included as a part of your work schedule.
- You need to make sure you (and your family) are worshipping at the church that employs you.

Your presence alone tells people, "I believe in this church and so should you."

If you aren't present at your parish on the weekends, people will question your ministry's integrity. It will be fair for them to question, "If this place isn't good enough for my youth minister, then is it good enough for me?"

I'll be honest; it is a challenge for me to give up a day on the weekend. It means shifting my days off, and I miss out on family events. It's a burden that my wife and I talk through constantly. Sometimes it's not an issue because we are both sold on the vision, but there are times when it just really stinks. The sacrifice is big, but it's worth it because it prevents a lot of frustration on a day-to-day basis.

When you are present on the weekends, you have a better shot at recruiting volunteers. You can connect with teens and the rest of the community. It says to everyone, including yourself, that you are present to the community for the highlight of its week. Your position becomes no longer just a job but grows into a calling.

Being present on the weekends can also make it difficult to truly worship and be spiritually fed. This is where it's important to set boundaries. When I'm at Mass with my family, the name tag comes off and I become a part of the congregation. Even if I'm serving as a Eucharistic minister, I'm doing it as Chris the parishioner and not the employee. There have been times when people come up to me in the middle of the liturgy to ask me about the Confirmation retreat. These are times when I need to tell them (with love), "Let's talk about this after Mass."

Again, worshipping where you work is a challenge and it is a sacrifice, but when you worship with the community you serve, you grow together because you are embarking on a spiritual journey together.

3. Connect with leaders in the parish.

Your sphere of influence is limited; therefore, networking is an important tool. Besides connecting on the weekends, connect with people in your parish who have a large circle of friends and

influence. These people will help you get the word out and introduce you to resources and people who are willing to invest. Start
out with your parish council and any other groups that are a part
of your church. Share with them the vision and mission of your
ministry. Invite them to check out what you do on a Sunday
night or whenever your groups meet. Sit with them and grow
with them relationally.

The more they get to know you, the more they will want to
assist you. They'll advocate in ways that you cannot. They'll refer
others interested in the youth ministry straight to you. They'll
have your back when the pressure is on, and they'll make your
ministry that much stronger.

Go beyond the youth room by making sure people are aware
of the teenagers in your community. If you focus on building
both a strong youth program and a vibrant youth presence across
all areas of parish life, you'll take your church to the next level
of discipleship. New life will be breathed in, and the energy it
produces will be contagious.

Part III

PLANNING FOR THE LONG HAUL

8

ACCEPT THE MESSINESS

I will rather boast most gladly of my weaknesses,
in order that the power of Christ may dwell with me.
Therefore, I am content with weaknesses, insults,
hardships, persecutions, and constraints, for the sake
of Christ; for when I am weak, then I am strong.
—2 Corinthians 12:9–10

On top of asking, "Why am I doing this?" you will ask yourself, at least once, "Can I keep on doing this?" Youth ministry can look simple from the outside. Many people think it's only about inviting teenagers to hang out, buying pizza, and planning fun. No one tells you how emotionally, spiritually, physically, and mentally exhausting it can be.

It doesn't matter how long you've been serving in the trenches of youth ministry, there will be times when it's no longer you but God's grace carrying you through. It's during these times when most people want to quit, shut down the program, and move on to something bigger or better. No matter how you try to approach or organize it, youth ministry is messy.

The first marathon I ever ran, I never finished. I had spent an entire year training, getting up early, changing my diet, and dedicating my mind, body, and soul—only to fall just two miles short of finishing. It wasn't that I gave up; it wasn't that it got too hard; I literally passed out from dehydration. That was something I thought I had control over. One minute I was running in this epic race, and the next minute the EMT was telling me to relax as the ambulance drove me to Maryland General Hospital in Baltimore.

The feelings that rushed through me were immense. I was embarrassed because family and friends had come to see me run. I was frustrated because a year of discipline and dedication was gone in an instant. I was disappointed because it was yet another thing that I had failed to complete. Let's just say I was down—way down.

Failure is something we all experience; it's unavoidable because we are human. One of the reasons many people and churches give up on youth ministry is because of the amount of disappointment and failure one can face.

You will pour so much energy into an event only to have just a few people show up. You will pull your hair out when a parent says, "I didn't get the e-mail," although you sent it out a dozen times. You will grow hopeless and helpless when men and women who said they would show up to volunteer are nowhere to be found.

I've struggled and failed so many times as a youth minister, I've lost count. I've made a teen sick during a game involving food consumption and left the church doors unlocked after a night of ministry. I've lost money on a fundraiser, unsuccessfully started up a college ministry three times, and ignored volunteers in need of my assistance. I've made mistakes, hit roadblocks, and come up empty. However, I've learned that it's okay to fail. In fact, failure can indeed build character when navigated well.

FAILURE IS PART OF THE JOURNEY

While I've made mistakes countless times, the one that sticks out the most is when I lost money on a fundraiser. In 2004, a major earthquake happened at the bottom of the Indian Ocean. The result was a massive tsunami and aftershocks that ravaged countries like Thailand and Indonesia. Our church responded immediately, sending a portion of our collection to those affected by this horrific event. High school students in our parish were very moved, and a few came to our pastor with the idea of holding a benefit concert. They were in a band and had friends with bands that had impressive followings. Our pastor agreed and they held the first "Be the Relief" concert. They were highly successful raising money and creating awareness. It was so popular that when Hurricane Katrina hit the Gulf Coast in 2005, they decided to duplicate the efforts. While the turnout was not as high as the first one, it was a hit among the youth. What made these events so successful was the emotion surrounding the cause and the fact that I was not involved. When the first two concerts took place, I was not a part of the planning or coordination because it was a high school event and I was the middle school youth minister. Looking back, I wish I had been more assertive with the planning stages.

Then about a year later, when I took over the high school youth ministry, students came to my office asking if we could do a third concert. I immediately panicked.

I don't know what your feelings are when it comes to event planning, but the idea of it makes me sweat. I'm not sure what it is about the logistics, but it's always overwhelming. I also didn't want to hurt the students' feelings. I was desperate for them to like me, so I reluctantly agreed to ask the pastor's permission.

I walked into his office, praying to God he would say, "Sorry, we've done two, no reason to do another." Instead he asked me if I was okay with it. Again I panicked; my mind shouted, "Say no!" but my mouth uttered, "Yeah, it'll be fine," and I walked out.

Now, I could have gone back into his office and said, "I'm sorry I misspoke," but the fear of letting down the students pushed me forward. I so desperately wanted them to like me. Despite feeling overwhelmed and unprepared, I continued on with the planning. The concert was always on my mind, but it was definitely not a top priority on my to-do list. Everything I did from vendors to volunteers was done at the last minute. I wasn't aggressive when it came to spreading the word because I assumed the bands had a large enough following. I treated the whole event as a burden instead of an opportunity. I prayed that the date would come soon, people would show, and then I could move on. The date came, but no one came; the event was a flop. Well, some people came, about three dozen—and that's a generous estimate—but it was bad. That night was long and painful. I went home, sick to my stomach, desperately worried about how I would face the pastor.

The next day as I walked into the office, our business manager, who could not have been more gracious, approached me. He informed me that we had lost $3,200 on the benefit concert. I wanted to hide under my desk; I had no idea how I would tell the pastor. So I didn't. I couldn't muster up the courage; I prayed the problem would just disappear. Of course he found out. Later that day, just as I was leaving, he came out of his office to confront me. I had never been reamed out like that before. I went home and cried.

I didn't know if I would have a job the next day, but instead of handing me a pink slip, the pastor forgave me. He said the reason he was so upset was how he had to find out about the concert's failure. He was confused as to why I didn't go to him or seek his help earlier. I learned from that moment that my pastor really cared about my success; he just didn't like hearing about my failures from other people. I learned a lot from that experience. One of the biggest takeaways was that I was still a worthwhile investment to my pastor.

Failure builds character because it takes you out of your comfort zone and begs you to grow. It frees you to discover your limits and your strengths. Failure is not always doom and gloom because no matter the outcome, God will always pick you up if you allow him to. Navigated well, failure can bring you:

1. Humility.

I was so worried about what others would think of me if I said no that I made a decision based on pride. Then, because I was reluctant to get my hands dirty, I was unable to put any real effort behind it. I made the whole process about me. Failure helps us realize that it's not supposed to be about us.

We don't need failure to find humility, but it will accelerate the process. It reminds us that what we do isn't about us first. Failure shows us that God has a plan and it doesn't matter how hard we push against it he will prevail. Humility is understanding that what God has in front of us is best for us and to fully embrace it, we need to work on our relationship with him.

To cultivate your humility, especially when facing failure, spend time examining where you sit with God. Do you trust him? If not, then what's holding you back? Failure reminds us to make decisions based on the plan God has for us. In fact, when we recognize that it's not about advancing our reputation but about God's glory, the possibilities are endless.

2. Growth.

While there was not a lot that I did right at first, I did walk away with a wealth of knowledge. That moment motivated me to embrace organizational disciplines and gave me strength to make the right decisions as opposed to the popular ones.

If you don't do something right the first time, failure will give you the opportunity to learn from your mistakes in the second go-round. When we succeed, we often forget to look at what makes us successful. Failure makes the situation a learning process. Failure brings us wisdom that can be passed on.

FIRST STEPS

Now, it's not about going out and trying to fail or creating messes just so you can learn. While failure can bring good things, it's not a habit you want to develop. Be sure to set high standards; strive to meet the vision of your ministry, your church, and what God has in store for your life. You just have to remember that you are always going to fall short of what God has prepared for you, but that doesn't mean you should dwell on the failure and messiness. Instead, it's important to know how to respond. When you fail, it's important to:

1. Acknowledge the failure.

The tendency is to deny failure and code it as a learning experience. While you can lie about failure, it isn't wise to live in denial. People will see through you and will question your competency. When you can acknowledge your shortcomings, you admit that there is a problem. A problem can be solved only if you are willing to admit it exists.

2. Take ownership.

Just as it's easy to deny failure, it's easy for us to point a finger and find a scapegoat. In the end, other people might have dropped the ball, or something out of your control may have caused a failure. If no one takes ownership, though, chances are high that the same thing will happen again. Failure is not the same as blame.

There was a time when I was pretty bad at writing questions for our small groups. I was asking too many close-ended questions, and the conversations would not flow. I had a few volunteers address the situation with me. Instead of accepting their feedback and advice, I blamed the teens. I told them that this was a rough bunch and that they didn't want to be there. Instead of listening to the wise counsel I was receiving and taking responsibility, I just blamed other people.

3. Seek insight and accountability.

Failure will challenge and bruise your ego. When this happens, it's very difficult to respond. While you might be determined to correct the situation on your own, it will be much easier to do this with someone helping you. After the experience, sit down with a trusted colleague who can share insight and encouragement. Allow him or her to point out what could have been avoided and what needs to be addressed. Having someone to lean on will make the healing process smoother.

4. Don't be afraid to fail again.

While you don't want to make the same mistakes, it's important not to fear failure. To get rid of the fear, hand it over to God. Allow him to take control and trust that he will continue to guide you toward your vision.

Failure can bring negative consequences. No one really aspires to be a failure, but always playing it safe can also bring trouble. Playing it safe by trying to please everyone and never striving to grow means a slow and painful death for your ministry. We aren't going to be able to save 100 percent of those we serve, but we can lose 100 percent if we don't take chances. If you fail, be humble and allow others to pick you up. People want a leader who's willing to risk failure and willing to seek help.

It took me a long time to recover mentally and emotionally from my marathon disaster. I remember feeling an overwhelming fear the next time I ran. The thoughts of, "Will I ever be able to do this?" "Am I risking injury?" and "Could I die?" raced through my mind. It was a moment of humility and clarity that led to immense growth. I realized no matter how much I studied or trained, running was a risk, but it was a risk worth taking. It was a risk that could lead to great satisfaction. There was a part of me that yearned to run, and to run far.

I had to embrace the fact that I didn't know everything, so I had to change my approach. That next year, I would attempt to run the marathon in the Baltimore Running Festival. The big difference this time was that I was more prepared for the pitfalls and obstacles that might stand in my way.

Youth ministry isn't comfortable or easy; otherwise everyone would do it. It should be filled with tension, and embracing it is tough. If you fail, get back up; if you get tired, rest; if you hit the wall, readjust. Remember that you are not alone.

I know some of you are wondering, "Chris, why designate a whole chapter to failure?" I wanted to address the reason many churches give up on youth ministry. While what we've learned at my parish has come from several youth ministry models, it's been tweaked, adjusted, and fitted for our unique parish. I cannot promise that everything we do will work in your paradigm, but that's okay. Try it out and make adjustments. If it fails, remember that it doesn't mean *you* are a failure.

Youth ministry can be frustrating because of the ever-changing landscape of adolescence. It can be hard when your pastor says no. It can be overwhelming when time and time again, no one shows up to volunteer. Youth ministry is hard and it's messy (messy, messy, messy) because that's the nature of humanity. It seems like a lot of work and a lot of risk, but for what?

I promise you that if you take on the challenge of serving the youth in your parish, the impact you'll have on God's kingdom is limitless. It's with young minds and hearts that you will find the courage to take on big problems. You are helping to unleash gifts and talents in your youth that have never been seen before because they are unique individuals living at this moment in the life of your parish and our Catholic Church.

Just keep learning, keep trying, and move on. I don't have all the answers—no one can—but I want to walk with you and share with you what I've learned over the years through good times and really messy ones.

9

KEEP ASKING THE RIGHT QUESTIONS

Do you not know that the runners in the stadium all run in the race, but only one wins the prize? Run so as to win.
—1 Corinthians 9:24

It may be that you're a pastor and a group of parents have approached you about starting a youth ministry. Maybe the church down the road has one and it's creating a positive buzz. Perhaps you are the new youth minister and you've been hired to breathe new life into a barely surviving program. Then again, you may have been in your position for a while now and are looking for some new direction or different approaches. It doesn't matter what the vision of your youth ministry is; if you don't know where you're starting (or where you are right now) you could find yourself heading in the wrong direction. Rebuilding a youth ministry is more than just setting a destination; it's about knowing the previous relationship your church has had with youth ministry, even if one never existed.

I had just been hired as the director of middle school youth ministry and it was my very first day on the job. Our student programs had not started up yet, but it was important for me to come in and get a feel for the weekend. No one really knew who

I was, although some may have realized I was a stranger. I walked around, observed, and just tried to soak it all in. The funny thing about first days is that it's all about assessing your situation. You want to impress people, but you also want to be as authentic and transparent as possible. I was a little overwhelmed, to say the least. I remember checking in with my pastor halfway through the day, only to be greeted by an entourage of high school altar boys. They asked me all sorts of questions and laughed at my responses. They weren't making fun of me; instead, it felt like they were sizing me up. I was the new guy on staff, they were going to have to work with me on the weekends, and they wanted to get a good sense of who I was. They wanted to know how long I would last in this place.

At lunch, I grabbed a slice of pizza and walked back to a room where volunteers could hang out in between Masses and during programs. I felt the same pressure a new kid does on his or her first day of school. I wanted people to like me because they could be future volunteers. I didn't want people wondering, "Why is he here?" I didn't want to draw too much attention to myself, and at the same time, I didn't want to be invisible. I tried to strike up as much small talk as I could so that I could learn more about others and the parish I was now serving. By the end of the day, I felt pretty welcomed and accepted.

I remember being exhausted and also grateful for surviving that first day. I had broken the ice and now thought I was ready to get the job done. The only problem—and it was considerable—was that I would have to figure out that first week pretty much on my own. My supervisor, Tom, was supposed to walk me through things and help acclimate me that week. Instead, he was away at a conference and his only instructions were, "Call these people on this list to ask them whether or not they'll lead small groups of students."

Talk about intimidating! Asking people I didn't know to volunteer for something I wasn't entirely clear about was a challenge, to say the least. Those were my instructions, though, and I faithfully and nervously followed them, calling every stranger on that list. All I got were voice mailboxes, and so I left awkward messages. When Tom returned he asked, "How did it go?" I honestly had absolutely no idea.

Anytime you do something new, it can feel rather surreal. You are stuck with wondering whether you are moving forward or just running in place. Looking back at that first week, I now know God wanted me to wait, look, and listen, but I didn't really get that then.

If you are starting out in youth ministry, looking to make drastic changes to one, or simply trying to grow a healthier version of yours, you need to understand the terrain. You need to understand the environments, events, and people who surround you. If you ignore where you are and what surrounds you, you won't be in ministry for long. Before you move into the journey and for as long as you continue along it, you need to start out by asking the right questions:

1. How does my parish see youth ministry?

This question is often overlooked. Just because your church hired you or asked you to start a youth ministry does not mean anyone knows what it is. After ten years, I still get asked by parents, teenagers, and random adults, "What is it you do?"

Your parish has an opinion of what a youth ministry should be; it just might not be accurate. According to *Renewing the Vision*, Catholic youth ministry has three goals:

- To empower young people to live as disciples of Jesus Christ in our world today.

- To draw young people to responsible participation in the life, mission, and work of the Catholic faith community.
- To foster the total personal and spiritual growth of each young person.[1]

For a variety of complex reasons, relatively few Catholic parishes know these goals or strive to reach them. Some churches have youth ministries that look more like adolescent babysitting, perpetual fundraisers, or teenage social hours. To achieve the goals laid out by the United States Conference of Catholic Bishops, you need to discover what your parish really knows about youth ministry. In other words, "Did the parish have a youth ministry before?" "What did it look like and was it successful?" If you are trying to grow an existing ministry, ask similar questions: "Which elements of our ministry are successful?" "How do we define success?" "Which ones need work?" "Do we have good vision and mission statements?"

Knowing the relationship your church had with youth ministry beforehand will help you understand why your position is stipend-based, full-, or part-time. It will help you see why certain programs and events are of high priority and others are not. It's also important to know why your pastor and the pastoral council want a youth ministry. Find out if your pastor and the council have had previous experience with youth ministry. If so, was it positive?

Learning how people in your parish—especially the leaders—see and define youth ministry will help you share your vision and mission. The difficulty about taking over a youth ministry is meeting, challenging, and changing expectations. You might discover that parents don't send their teenager because their kid already takes religion class at the local Catholic school. Teens might have no interest in going because they believe it's a place where all the social outcasts go. Adults might be reluctant to volunteer if they think it's beneath them because all you do is serve pizza. People might turn down your invitations to volunteer because they think they have to be theologians and they feel inadequate.

Discern what parishioners think and use the vision and mission to help them change their perception. It will take time; however, the more they see what God is doing with the youth in your parish, the more they'll want to invest in it.

2. Who are the people I'm inheriting?

The work is hard enough if you are new to youth ministry, and it's even more difficult if you are new to the parish that employs you. A new parish means not having any idea who is competent, dependable, or has potential leadership abilities. To figure out whom you need on your team, you need to make relationship building a priority.

I spent the majority of my first year meeting one-on-one with the leaders I inherited. It wasn't anything fancy; I just went out for coffee or a bite to eat and said, "Tell me about yourself." There was no planned questionnaire or agenda; it was an opportunity to get to know them and have them get to know me. It was during those times that I learned whom I could lean on for ministry and even personal matters.

If the team you inherit is small, meeting with volunteers outside of the youth ministry setting will give you better insight into their overall character. Once you've broken the ice, you can begin to take small risks by giving them responsibility and ownership of a project or activity. Then you'll want to observe how they work with others, problem-solve, and deal with unexpected pressures. When you are getting started, it's easier to observe how people will handle certain roles because you haven't established any emotional attachments to programs or structures. You can be more objective.

If the team you inherit is big, see if you can get recommendations from the pastor, coworkers, or even the former youth minister about the people you should talk with. Instead of feeling like you have to meet everyone, start with those who are commonly recognized as leaders. Once you've established who your leaders are, they will help you with the rest.

No matter the size of the team you inherit, as you get more comfortable you'll discover who is on board and who is out of place. You might not know what to do with them; however, just keep track of how they are leading and interacting with your team. Although this is the team you are inheriting, it doesn't mean they have to be the team that stays with you forever. While you don't want to go in right away and take out what was put in place before, know that you do have the right and responsibility to surround yourself with the best people to help you do the best you can in your ministry.

Nothing can be scarier than volunteers leaving before you even get started. Do not be alarmed if there is high turnover at the beginning. Just as you are scouting out their talent, they are doing the same. It's probably not that they don't like you, so don't take it personally. Very often volunteers see staff or leadership transitions as a good opportunity for them to get out of a commitment and move on to something new.

3. What deserves to die and what needs to stay?

My first project as a youth minister was planning a crab feast for the middle school program. This is a Maryland tradition where we order bushels of crabs—about six or seven dozen—and cook them up to enjoy at an outdoor gathering. If you've never eaten crabs right from the shell, let me tell you it can be a lot of work—at least the way people do this in Baltimore. A true crab aficionado needs only a plastic knife to pull apart the complex crustacean.

However, if you are just getting started, my recommendation is to have a small wooden mallet to break the shells, along with plenty of newspaper and paper towels. To enjoy the delicious crabmeat, you are forced to pry away layers upon layers of hard crab shell. Despite all the hard work, your reward is the equivalent of a tablespoon of crabmeat. It's a lot of effort for little reward, but everyone in Maryland seems to love this.

As a guy from New Jersey, I had no clue what was involved in planning a true crab feast. What I learned right off the bat, the hard way, is that planning a crab feast requires finding someone to transport the crabs for you. No matter what I tried, the stench of seafood and Old Bay Seasoning lingered in my car for months. Despite the smelly mess and difficult extraction of the meat, the crab feast was a lot of fun. It was a great chance to meet the teens and to get to know the leaders. Everyone was excited to be there, and it really did serve as a landmark event to start off the year. Despite its popularity, this event bore little fruit for the health and longevity of the greater program. From the beginning, it was apparent I couldn't cancel it right away; I needed to let it run for one more year before announcing the decision. The event had run its course. To my surprise, the pushback I received was minimal because people seemed to understand my reasons. Unfortunately that wasn't the case for other programs and events I eventually had to kill.

Programs in your ministry can easily become sacred cows. People will plead with you and try to convince you that you are making a huge mistake by getting rid of them. After you kill off a program, or even announce its end, be prepared to receive phone calls, e-mails, and even face-to-face confrontation. People will take it personally, so don't be surprised if they go directly to your pastor. Even if it is blatantly obvious to you why you should get rid of the program, expect people to push back on your decisions.

To know which ones to keep and which ones to kill, you need to look at whether or not the fruit outweighs the labor. In other words, is the payoff worth all the work and energy you pour into a specific project or event? As you establish a vision and mission, you'll want to make sure they run parallel with all the events and programs in your ministry. If it's not obvious and you are unsure about its future, take your time and take thoughtful steps before eliminating it.

4. What does God need me to do?

Starting out, you may know why you got into ministry. But do you know what it is God wants you to do now that you're there? I had an idea of what I wanted to do when I first started; I wanted to create a ministry more entertaining and engaging than what I grew up with. I wanted a place where all teenagers were accepted and no one was rejected. I would plan awesome events and really cool programs—that was my plan.

Eight months into ministry, my church sent Maria, the high school youth minister at the time, two of our volunteers and me to the Purpose Driven Youth Ministry Conference at Saddleback Church in Lake Forest, California. Saddleback is Rick Warren's (author of *The Purpose Driven Life*) church, an Evangelical congregation. I remember being confused as to what I could possibly learn at the conference. What more was there to youth ministry besides planning a few events for teens to come to and showing them that church can be fun? On the way from the airport to where we were staying, I remember telling Maria about my skepticism, joking about and judging something I didn't even know.

That conference changed me forever. Through various keynote speakers who shared their "in the trenches" youth ministry stories and the music that helped us to focus and surrender to God, I began to realize that youth ministry is something much more than I first thought. There was no pinnacle moment that week; it's just as if one idea after another clicked during each breakout and main session I attended. During that conference, I remember feeling like God was pulling on my heart and telling me that he had big plans for me. That night, I knew my ministry would be something more than just a temporary job. I dug in and started asking more of the right questions more of the time.

FIRST STEPS

It doesn't matter if you have been in youth ministry for thirty seconds or thirty years, it's important for you to check in from time to time to witness the progress you've made in your journey. To make sure you are constantly asking the right questions:

1. Seek outside insight.

Over time you'll find yourself so immersed in the trenches of youth ministry that you will lose sight of what is important. To make sure you are consistently growing your youth ministry, look to outside perspectives to hold you accountable.

Surrounding yourself with the right people is important. Going to friends, coworkers, other parish leaders or staff, and your pastor is an effective way of gaining insight. Two groups of people I would highly recommend adding to that list are other youth ministers and new volunteers.

- **Learn from other youth ministers.** There is nothing more humbling or intimidating than inviting youth ministers from other churches (Catholic or not) to come in and observe your ministry. Invite them to ask questions and to pick apart what you do. Before you become overly sensitive, remember they'll understand your battles and approach you with the love you deserve.

- **Learn from new volunteers.** New volunteers are not battle-tested. They are also not jaded by the experience that you have. What they provide for you is a whole new perspective. We gather a group of new volunteers three to six months after they begin serving to get an honest assessment of what they see. We encourage them to ask questions and give frank input. It's amazing what a fresh set of eyes will expose for you.

By gaining outside insight you'll learn why people leave or are not coming. You will discover what works and what needs to be tweaked. There will be some insight you can dismiss, but mostly there will be a lot of fresh perspective on the truth to help you out.

2. Study trends.

Your youth ministry does not exist in a vacuum. It's easy to arrive at a certain point and stay there because you feel comfortable, but the world is constantly changing around you. It's important that you stay on top of trends in the ministry because they will affect your ministry (like it or not).

Subscribe to websites that review trends (e.g., Mashable.com), read magazines (usually the ones you find in the checkout aisle in a supermarket), and poll your middle school students (they have less of a filter than high school students). Do not be afraid to engage and lean into what the culture is throwing at you. Studying the trends will force you to ask questions about your ministry's relevancy.

3. Revisit your vision and mission statements.

A question that will sneak constantly into your mind and heart is, "Why am I doing this?" Revisiting your vision and mission will help you assess whether or not you've stayed on the right track.

Both vision and mission can serve as anchors that will help you determine whether a program has lost relevancy. It will help you determine the effectiveness of your systems.

Our leadership team gets together each year to look at what we are doing and why what we are doing matters. It allows us to take a step back and answer that question, "Why?" It prevents us from becoming too comfortable and complacent with how we are functioning.

Youth ministry in the Catholic Church is still a new profession that is constantly changing and evolving. When I was in high school, most youth ministers were volunteers, priests, deacons, or poorly paid college students. Today, it is slowly turning into a dynamic, vibrant, essential ministry in many parishes. Young men and women are now majoring in it at college and making the conscious decision that this is what God is calling them to do full-time.

Because youth ministry is new, what you may have experienced as a teenager doesn't have to determine the way you do things today. In fact, it probably shouldn't. It doesn't matter how long you've been in ministry; don't stop asking the right questions. Address the misperceptions, look at the people who surround you, and evaluate the programs you've inherited. It will help you see what God is calling you to do.

10

BECOME AND REMAIN A LEARNING, GROWING MINISTRY

^

Therefore, my beloved brothers, be firm, steadfast, always fully devoted to the work of the Lord, knowing that in the Lord your labor is not in vain.
—1 Corinthians 15:58

Youth ministry can easily be confused with event planning. Events are a quick path to drawing large numbers. When people see a crowd, they will assume that you have a vibrant and healthy youth ministry. While numbers do indicate success, they are not always a sign of health and not the only indicator of success. It's dangerous to rely only on the numbers. Every youth ministry needs to grow in number but also in depth of discipleship formation.

While retreats and events have the ability to inspire someone toward Christ, they can help someone go only so deep. In the end, there needs to be a next step. Events and retreats should serve as a catalyst in a young person's life. If all you do is plan events and retreats, you'll find yourself growing consumers of feel-good events and burning yourself out.

When I was in high school, I was a bit of a retreat junky. I attended anywhere from three to four weekend church retreats a year. You might think, "Wow, he must have really loved church." The reality is that it was a great way of making new friends and there was always at least one cute girl going. (What can I say? I was a teenage boy.)

There was nothing unique about these retreats; in fact, that's one of the reasons I went. They all had the same talks. The first one of the weekend was about tearing away the masks that prevented us from showing others who we really were. That would lead into more messages about teenage angst. Just when you thought your life was filled with drama, here was a teenager who made yours look like an episode of *Full House*.

As the weekend continued, there would be highs and lows of emotion. The pinnacle was during Saturday night's reconciliation service. At this point, everyone was convinced of his or her sinful nature. The adults would encourage us to write it down on a sheet of paper and give it up in a burnt offering. The night was filled with tears, sobs, and moments of, "I love you, man."

At the end of the weekend, after being torn down and built back up, we would attend Mass with our families. After Communion, we all had the opportunity to share our testimonies. During that time there were really powerful moments when teens would share their newfound love for Christ. Other participants who weren't as comfortable with the emotion would share an inside joke for a laugh. Then the testimonies would conclude with the chant of the name of the quiet teen. This was probably the most awkward moment because the reluctance on that person's face was obvious. The pressure was immense and to ignore your name being chanted over and over again would have been social suicide. After being bullied into going up, the teen would most likely make the comment, "Thanks for everything, guys. Love you," followed by everyone's cheers.

As cheesy as it seems, looking back on those experiences, I loved them and could never get enough of them. This became a problem as each retreat concluded. Despite feeling spiritually fulfilled, I was emotionally drained. It didn't matter how many talks I heard about living out the retreat in our everyday lives. Getting over the emotions was a detoxification process. I would be miserable the next day and so would everyone around me. The spiritual high was so good, so real, but never sustainable. Leaders would pour all their energy and resources into providing an *emotional* experience. Sometimes the only purpose of the retreat was to provoke a tear, a regret, or a moment of guilt. Many of the adult leaders wanted an emotional response because it was a tangible, concrete sign—of what, I'm not sure.

Looking back, I see many of the benefits these church retreats had on my life. Through them I met my closest friends, I was able to escape the chaos of my parents' divorce, and I did learn more about God. They never did prepare me for life outside of the retreat, though. After a week or two, the confidence, support, and love that I had received were gone.

I don't have a problem with retreats. If done right they can be an empowering and faith-changing experience. I just don't think they can be the only thing or *the* thing that makes your ministry what it is. The issue with making retreats the pinnacle of your youth ministry is that they are not consistent. This is true for other events as well. We look to them to be the quick fix to instant success.

Our goal as youth ministers needs to be creating consistent opportunities, environments, and relationships that are going to help teens grow in their faith. It's just like any relationship you want to take to a deeper level; you need to consistently communicate and meet with that person if you want to have a more personal and authentic relationship. It's the same with working out; you know that you don't get in shape by doing push-ups once a week. Your spiritual health is the same as your physical health. In order to grow disciples who are healthy, you need to give them consistent opportunities to learn about Christ and grow in their relationships with other Christians.

In our student ministry, we look not only at what we are teaching but at how it's delivered. Our main delivery method of God's truth is through our middle school and high school programs. We give them distinct names, and they are grouped like this:

- **Resurrection** is for sixth through eighth graders and it meets Sunday evenings from 6:30 to 8:15.
- **Uprising** is for high school students and it meets Thursday evenings from 7:00 to 9:00.

Why those programs meet at those times and where they meet are all due to strategic decisions based on our campus limitations. Unfortunately, we don't have the space at the ideal times for our program. Ideally, I would like to have our middle school and high school programs meet at the same time. This would prevent families from making multiple trips and cut down on the use of our resources. Right now, these are the next best times for our ministry paradigm.

Our high school program used to meet on Sunday evenings, but we found that Thursday provided us a better opportunity to engage our teens and meet our goals. Thursday gives us a better shot at preparing them for the weekend and gives them a mile-marker in their week. Picking the best time and place is essential, but if it isn't consistent you'll never find momentum. So decide on a time and place and stick with it.

Each week teenagers can walk into our program and expect:

- An environment where they are welcomed and loved for who they are, despite what they know or their beliefs
- An activity or game that will encourage them to open their minds
- Music to help them worship God or reflect on what's going on in their lives
- A fifteen-minute message designed just for them that will let them hear how God works in their lives
- Small groups where they will meet with their peers and two adults who want to walk with them in this season of their faith journey

Once in a while, we'll have different elements and variations of those five components. However, each week from July until May, that's pretty much what you can expect from us. Is it the only way to do ministry? Probably not, but it's what is working for us right now. Some people might ask, "How is it possible to run a ministry that meets on a weekly basis for eleven months out of the year?" Let me tell you.

FIRST STEPS

Before you announce to your parish, "We're starting a youth ministry," make sure you prepare the foundation so that as each season approaches, your ministry can face the challenges life will bring it. Make sure you do the following:

1. Design a program that is sustainable.

A sustainable program means doing the one thing only you can do on a consistent basis. For me, that's meeting with a small group of teens regularly. I know if all else fails, I can just sit down with the teens in my ministry, pray with them, listen to them tell me about their lives, and talk to them about Jesus Christ. Once you find what a stripped-away, bare-bones youth ministry looks like, you then need to:

2. Pick a day and time that works.

You aren't going to pick the perfect day for everyone. To pick the best one, you need to make sure you talk with parents, teenagers, and your pastor. Our days and times aren't ideal, but we found they work because parents have enough time to pick up their teens from whatever activity they were involved in after school and drive them over to the church. No matter what day and time you meet, make sure it's clear and consistent. If you announce that you begin at 6:30, make sure you are ready to go at 6:15. If you are scheduled to end at 8:30, make sure you end at 8:30. Consistency is the key to excellence and trust.

To run a consistent ministry can be overwhelming, but it is also very doable. To make sure you stay consistent, you need to have people around you to encourage you and hold you accountable. In fact, youth ministry should never be done alone. That is why, to equip your ministry, you need to:

3. Recruit people who see the big picture.

It's one thing for you, the youth minister, to commit to weekly service. To get other people to serve once a week might seem like an impossible task. When it comes to finding ministers who will consistently serve in your student ministry, you need to paint for them a clear vision. You need to explain to them how this will influence not only the lives of young people but their own lives as well. People who see the vision and embrace it will not be deterred by a once-a-week commitment; in fact, we have found some people will give you even more than you ask.

It's also important not to settle for just anyone. You need the right people on board to make your ministry grow.

4. Begin with a test group.

When we built our small-group program, we had our leaders and teens commit to only six weeks in the fall and then six weeks in the spring (during Lent). With a less daunting commitment, people were more enthusiastic about jumping on board. After going through it once, we had sufficient time to analyze and review the entire program. The following year, we built it up to eight weeks in the fall and eight weeks in the spring. The year after that, it was eight weeks in the fall and ten in the spring. At that point, we took the jump to go year-round.

With the right people on board and a system in place, we were able to build a strong and healthy program. The numbers were nothing to brag about, but we were fulfilling our vision of growing disciples and making church matter.

5. Make adjustments along the way.

When it comes to creating consistent programming, you will never be finished. In order to stay strong, you need to constantly analyze and make sure everything is still flowing correctly. To tweak, adjust, and improve your ministry, ask these three questions:

- **Does this fulfill our purpose?** You will grow comfortable with how you do ministry and discover that some programs have lost their appeal. The next step is to examine how to bring your ministry to the next level. You can do that by revisiting your mission and determining whether or not you are still fulfilling the purpose. In our case, we need to examine whether or not we are still leading teenagers to be authentic, consistent, and irresistible examples of Jesus Christ. If you stray away from your purpose, you'll find yourself running around in circles until you burn out.
- **Is this a competing system?** It's good to have a competitive spirit. It allows you to be aggressive in your

strategy. However, when you start planning programs that compete with other programs in your church or ministry, you'll find only frustration. When this happens, you'll need to look at whether your programs need to be tweaked, refocused, or possibly eliminated. When you have competing systems, you exhaust yourself and your resources. It will create animosity in the staff culture, and in the end no one wins.

- **Does the labor outweigh the fruit?** Sometimes you might feel inclined to do more with your program. It could work and be well-received, but the amount of time you put into it might outweigh the benefits. Again, revisit whether or not what you are doing is sustainable and then scale back. This can be painful because it can involve eliminating something you have cherished and championed.

The key to a long-lasting ministry is consistency and commitment. Events, retreats, and gatherings can all have a positive impact; they just can't be the be-all and end-all. If you love events, use them to jump-start the flow of your consistent program. Use them as the hook to draw teenagers into something that they will consistently enjoy and come back to. If you have a retreat, make sure teens have a resource, like a devotional, to help them process the experience. Establishing a consistently learning, growing ministry is a challenging commitment, but in the end only by doing so will you be able to reach goals and move closer to your vision.

POSTSCRIPT
YOU AND I WERE BORN FOR THIS

So, why am I a youth minister? The answer is simple—that's what God has called me to do. I don't know what he has in store for me over the next few years, but I look forward to them. It's been an amazing journey thus far, and I know what lies ahead is only greater. I know there will be moments of pain, doubt, and fear; nevertheless, the hope I have for God's promise will pull me through. The memories and relationships built along the way have been and will continue to be priceless. Youth ministry is a long journey, and it's totally worth it.

My adolescence, although difficult, was filled with so many wonderful moments and people. From the middle school youth minister who I drove crazy to the three parents, Rob, Lynnie, and Judi, who just gave me so much of their love and time, I have been richly blessed. Without their sacrifices, my life and the lives of other teenagers would never have been changed for the better.

In college, I found a Jesuit priest by the name of Father Bischoff. He invested in me and allowed me to bring anything to him. He was my spiritual mentor and one of the main reasons I followed God's calling to Baltimore, where my life as a youth minister, a husband, and a father would begin. Throughout my life, there have been men and women in the Church who have shown me what it means to be a disciple of Christ. It's because of their ministry to the next generation that I was able to find Christ and a love for the Church.

When you have those days, weeks, months, or years when you question whether or not this is worth it, remember the impact you can have. You'll probably see that most clearly in the little things. This note I received from a parent about one of our small-group leaders helps me remember the good God does through my ministry.

> Hi Chris. Since none of the other girls in Leslie's small group were able to attend the high school program last night, Tina asked Leslie if she still wanted to meet. They ended up taking our dog for a walk for over an hour and talked about "everything," according to Leslie. I just wanted you to know that I think it's great that this relationship Tina has established with Leslie and the other girls reaches into their lives and isn't only at church.

What was particularly awesome about receiving this e-mail was the fact that when Leslie and the rest of her small-group members were introduced to Tina, they were not very pleased. To them, Tina wasn't cool or hip enough to be their leader. Four years later as I was saying good-bye to this group, one of them came up to me and said, "Tina is *our* small-group leader; we do not want her to be anyone else's." Tina was not only a role model for these girls but also an example of Christ. It's because of Tina that these girls know that God is always near and available for them.

When those moments happen, cherish them. Maybe that's hard for you because you've recently failed. Maybe you just feel worn-out and tired. I get it; I've been there and will probably find myself there again. It's easy to be your own biggest critic, but that's just Satan trying to knock you down. No matter what you are thinking, remember that you, like me, were born for this!

If you are a pastor or parish life director reading this book, remember the man or woman you've charged with this responsibility is fighting the battle with you. By understanding how to empower, invest in, and cheer that person on during this journey, you not only will build a long-lasting youth ministry but you also will find a trusted companion. My pastor has invested greatly in me; he's allowed me to take risks and challenge him. It's one of the fundamental reasons I've been in the same church for over a decade.

For those of you in the trenches, don't ever forget why God has called you to youth ministry. Remember you are not alone and you aren't the first one to go on this journey. Again, it is a journey; it will not happen overnight. There are people cheering for you, excited to see how you will grow. There are people willing to help you up, refuel you, and carry you forward. Youth ministry can be grueling, but it's worth it. The next time doubt fills your mind and you wonder, "Why do something that people don't consider a real job for which I am underpaid and overworked?" "Why invest in teens, parents, and people who disappoint me and let me down?" "Why invest in a career that can feel like an island?" remember the answer is *life change*. You are a youth minister because God has called you to create opportunities, relationships, and environments that will lead to life change. That life change will affect not only the lives of young people but also the future of the Church. You are leading the pack, so enjoy and embrace it. Celebrate those wins, recognize you will fall, but never forget the vision God has instilled in you. If it hadn't been for men and women like you, I wouldn't be nearly as blessed as I am today. Thank you for all you do to make church matter to the young people you serve and so build up the Body of Christ.

NOTES

1. Make It Way More Than Pizza

1. Mary Elizabeth Carrol, "Bishop Sheil: Prophet Without Honor," *Harper's Magazine*, November 1955.

2. Michael White and Tom Corcoran, *Rebuilt: Awakening the Faithful, Reaching the Lost, and Making Church Matter* (Notre Dame, IN: Ave Maria Press, 2013), 72.

3. Andy Stanley, Reggie Joiner, and Lane Jones, *7 Practices of Effective Ministry* (Colorado Springs, CO: Multnomah, 2004), 70.

4. Doug Fields, *Purpose Driven Youth Ministry: 9 Essential Foundations for Healthy Growth* (Grand Rapids, MI: Zondervan, 1998), 73–74.

2. Pursue Authentic Relationships with Small Groups and Mentors

1. United States Conference of Catholic Bishops, *Renewing the Vision: A Framework for Catholic Youth Ministry* (Washington DC: USCCB Publishing, 1997), 13.

4. Clarify Your Message

1. Ibid., 29.

2. Michael White and Tom Corcoran, *Tools for Rebuilding: 75 Really, Really Practical Ways to Make Your Parish Better* (Notre Dame, IN: Ave Maria Press, 2013), 124.

7. Go Beyond the Youth Room

1. USCCB, *Renewing the Vision*, 16–17.

9. Keep Asking the Right Questions

1. USCCB, *Renewing the Vision*, Vol. 6, 22.

Christopher Wesley is director of student ministry at Church of the Nativity in Timonium, Maryland. He is also team leader for the parish's family ministry programs and serves on the pastor's strategic leadership team. He is active with unCUFFed Ministries in Baltimore. Wesley writes the *Marathon Youth Ministry blog* (christopherwesley.org), is the host of the weekly Rebuilt podcast, and writes content for downloadyouthministry.com.

Wesley has a bachelor's degree in communication arts, electronic media, from Xavier University in Cincinnati, Ohio. A native of Mountain Lakes, New Jersey, Chris has lived in Tokyo; Hong Kong; Auckland, New Zealand; Cincinnati; and Baltimore. He and his wife, Katherine, have two sons.